50 THINGS TO DO IN DUBLIN

An Insider's Guide

Michael Barry

Published by DMCRS Ltd
for DCBA Ltd

DMCRS Ltd, 21 Dawson Street, Dublin 2, Ireland. *info@dcba.ie*

Book layout and text: Michael Barry.
Cover and template design: Anú Design.
Printer: Printer Trento Srl, Italy.
ISBN: 97809571864-0-8

2012 EDITION

DUBLIN
WOOLLEN
MILLS

Introduction

You are in Dublin. You have just negotiated Dublin airport, sampled the taxi-driver's wit and beaten the traffic into the city. You are in your hotel. Now you are here – what to do? You want to capture the essence of this city, get the best from it, whether for a few days or much longer. This book is designed for you.

Dublin is an accessible city. You can walk around the central area quite easily and see many interesting sights. Its rich history has shaped the city in a distinctive manner. There is superb heritage – all over are great, good and interesting buildings. There is culture (art galleries, literature, plus theatre and music). Ireland and Dublin are different, and possess a special originality. This quirkiness is what produced a host of great writers who interpreted life and the English language in an equally quirky manner, with benefits to world culture: Oscar Wilde; James Joyce; George Bernard Shaw, Seán O'Casey, Brendan Behan and Samuel Beckett.

Dublin (and Ireland) have all the accolades, (UNESCO City of Literature, Europe's friendliest place) but let's get real here. This is not a city running like a Swiss clock (sorry, Switzerland). Sometimes it's a bit chaotic. However, what raises the city above the ordinary are the people: they will engage with you. This is a social city. They are a friendly bunch, the Dubliners. They will talk to you. In a pub, shop, or on a bus they will have a conversation. In this vibrant, lively city, they will be (generally) helpful, sharp and witty.

As globalisation becomes the norm, and differences fall away, Dublin, whilst a capital city, still keeps its uniqueness and operates to its own rhythm. There is a huge variety of things to see. In overall terms, this is a gem among European cities, well worth the trouble to get to know. Dublin has depth and soul, and, in the Spanish sense of magical quality, *duende*. It's not huge but it's a great city.

This book is intended to give you a flavour of the best of Dublin. It is divided into broad geographical areas (central Dublin, etc), to make it easy to navigate. Additionally, 10 places near Dublin, worth visiting, are listed. This is a new book, written by someone who lives in the city, and this knowledge allows, as well as the usual sights, the inclusion of interesting areas where, hitherto, not many tourists have ventured.

When anyone visits a city, they want to see what is unique, what can't be seen in other places: this book lists these as ★★. These are special, distinctive to Dublin. Try to see them. Other great places that are very worthwhile and that merit your time are listed as ★. Take this book, visit, look, see, engage, meet and talk, and above all, enjoy this wonderful city.

Fáilte go Baile Átha Cliath!

Orientation

The River Liffey bisects and defines the city, flowing from its source high in the Wicklow Mountains to run from west to east through the city and into Dublin Bay. The Royal Canal swings around the north of the centre. The Grand Canal loops around to the south. These form an oval shape, which was mainly the 18th-century city. Outside the canals is an intermediate necklace of red-brick Victorian suburbs, surrounded in turn by 20th-century buildings.

It could be said that the General Post Office (GPO), north of the river, is at the heart of the city, marked by the adjacent stainless steel spire. This is on the main thoroughfare, O'Connell St, which runs south to O'Connell Bridge. South of the Liffey are most of the central sights such as Dublin Castle, Trinity College and the National Museum, Library and Gallery. There are good shopping areas in and around the Grafton St area. To simplify, and this is a source of some sensitivity and dispute, it could be said that the central area north of the river has a grittier feel, while south of the river is perceived as 'posher'. Dublin is more than the centre, however, and dotted all around are wonderful places to visit, as seen in the list of things to do in this book.

Dublin, as befits a medieval city, has developed in fits and starts, and this has left its stamp with its geographical spread. The first significant Viking settlement was on high ground roughly between present-day Dublin Castle and the river. Over the centuries, the city developed around that area. During the 18th century there was great growth and the city expanded north of the river. As the Parliament Building on College Green and Leinster House were built, the city developed on the south side. By 1801 the city had grown to be, after London, the second city of the kingdom. However, after the Act of Union, growth slackened. The central city entered a period of stasis. The middle classes fled from the centre and the Victorian suburbs sprang up, first in the south, then in other areas. The 20th century saw urban sprawl and growth to over one million people. The present century brought rapid building which has now come to a halt.

Note: Entrance fees/tour prices shown are adult prices. Check admission times as these may change.

Contents

Central Dublin

Contents

Around Dublin

Key:

★★ Unique/exceptional, must see

★ Worthwhile, enjoyable

Contents

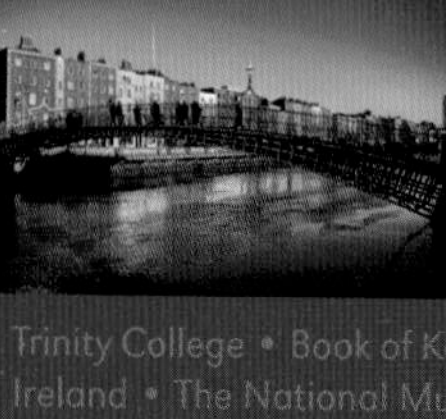

Trinity College • Book of Kells • Dublin Castle • Chester Beatty Library • Two and
Ireland • The National Museum • The National Library • Dublinia • Literary Du
Green • The Hugh Lane Gallery • By Appointment • Guinness Storehouse • Old
Theatre • Trinity College • Book of Kells • Dublin Castle • Chester Beatty Library
Gallery of Ireland • The National Museum • The National Library • Dublinia •
Green • The Hugh Lane Gallery • Guinness Storehouse • Old Jameson Distillery
College • Book of Kells • Dublin Castle • Chester Beatty Library • Two and a H

Dublin

Central Dublin

thedrals • Marsh's Library • Natural History Museum • The National Gallery of
es Joyce • Dublin Writers Museum • City Hall • Merrion Square • St Stephen's
Distillery • Gandon on the Liffey • Dublin Music • Temple Bar • 1916 Walk •
a Half Cathedrals • Marsh's Library • Natural History Museum • The National
ublin • James Joyce • Writers Museum • City Hall • Merrion Square • St Stephen's
on the Liffey • Dublin Music • Temple Bar • 1916 Walk • Theatres • Trinity
drals • Marsh's Library • Natural History Museum

01 Trinity College

View from Front Square

One of the oldest universities in Western Europe, Trinity College (Dublin University) was founded in 1592 by a charter of Queen Elizabeth I. Her intention was to spread Protestantism in Ireland. The university grew and by the mid-19th century it was bigger than Oxford University. Originally it mainly catered for the Protestant Ascendancy. Paradoxically, Catholics were prohibited from attending the university by the Catholic Church, a rule which lasted to 1970. Now there are around 17,000 students, of all religions and none. Former students include Oliver Goldsmith, Edmund Burke, Oscar Wilde, Samuel Beckett and Bram Stoker (author of *Dracula*).

The main entrance is at College Green. Walk through the front gate and enter into Front Square. It is a centre of tranquillity, learning and great architecture, a nearly 20-hectare world away from the bustle of central Dublin.

Grey, classical, elegant, Front Square is flanked by the Chapel (northern side) and the Examination Hall (southern side). Sit on the steps of the Dining Hall which adjoins the Chapel and savour this true grove of academia. The Campanile (dating from 1853) gives a focus to the square. Observe the flurry of students bustling around between lectures or heading to the library. In today's harsher world, most students take their studies seriously.

Behind the campanile is the Library Square. Look out for the Henry Moore sculpture. On the south side is the imposing Old Library which dates from 1733.

Continue eastwards into New Square. Immediately to the south is the (depending on your taste) 'new brutalism' or the outstanding concrete facade of the Berkeley Library, which dates from 1967. There is a great contrast betwen this and the Museum Building, which is to the east of the Berkeley Library. This was completed in 1857 by the brilliant architectural duo of Deane and Woodward. In grey stone, it brings Venice to this academic setting. Walk around and observe the exquisite stone carvings, executed by the duo's favourite stone carvers, who included the O'Shea brothers. (See also carvings by the same ensemble, at Kildare St, p.25.) The interior is eclectic: a giant Irish deer on display; a soaring Byzantine entrance hall with rich and exquisite carvings in stone.

Walk behind the Museum Building to the south and the college develops an almost sylvan character. Students engage in athletic events on the playing fields, as the traffic roars along Nassau St.

Museum Building

College Green, D2
☎*01 8962320*
www.tcd.ie
Book of Kells exhibition times:
Mon-Sat 9.30am-5pm
Sun 9.30am-4.30pm, May-Sept. From 12am, Oct-Apr
Admission: €9
Getting there: Take Nassau St entrance, the Old Library entrance is directly ahead.

Book of Kells

One of the most popular exhibitions in Dublin, this is an opportunity to see one of the most important (and oldest) books in the world. The Book of Kells dates from the early 9th century. Produced by monks on the island of Iona (off the coast of Scotland), who moved to Kells in County Meath, after a Viking raid. It contains the four gospels in Latin and depicts wonderful illuminated Celtic designs. Other manuscripts are also on display.

Exit is via the Long Room. This building, much modified in the mid-19th century, has an impressive 65m long chamber. It houses 200,000 of the Library's oldest books. Exhibits include the oldest surviving harp in Ireland.

The Long Room

02 Dublin Castle

Left: Bedford Tower; Right: Statue of Justice

Dublin Castle has, over the centuries, been the centre of control of the country. You can experience the full range of Ireland's history, from the Vikings to the present day, in this wonderful enclave.

The Norman King John ordered the construction of the castle in 1204. During the reign of Queen Elizabeth I, the struggle for control of Ireland resulted in members of the native Irish aristocracy being incarcerated here. Red Hugh O'Donnell, son of an important Donegal chieftain, made his escape from here twice, in 1591 and 1592. Rebel heads were often displayed on spikes on the castle walls.

There were efforts by rebels to capture the castle, a very visible symbol of foreign dominance. Robert Emmet planned to take it during his failed 1803 rebellion. During the 1916 Rising, there was a skirmish here on Easter Monday when members of the Citizen Army attempted to occupy the castle. A key part of Irish history occurred in 1922, when the Viceroy handed over the castle to Michael Collins, who represented the nascent Irish state.

Entering the castle at the upper gate, past City Hall, a statue of Justice is seen over the gate. She faces the castle, resulting in local wits saying that she had turned her back on the city. The Bedford Tower is to the immediate right in the upper yard. Designed by Thomas Eyre around 1750, it has a copper dome. The statue of Fortitude is nearby. This was the scene of a great unsolved mystery: the Irish crown jewels were stolen from here in 1907 and never recovered. On the south of the upper yard are the State Apartments (see panel for details of tour).

On state occasions, the upper yard is a swirl of colour and pageant with military guards of honour and ceremonial arrivals of the President and foreign heads of state.

Passing into the lower castle yard, the Record Tower is to the right. Originally a prison, it was from here that Red Hugh O'Donnell escaped. Adjacent to the tower is the Chapel Royal, a delightful Gothic jewel of a church to a design by Francis Johnston, which opened in 1814. There is a profusion of carved stone heads around the building. Inside is an impressive depiction of the centuries of foreign rule: the arms of the viceroys from 1172 to 1922 are on display.

Continue down the lower yard and to the right. Pass some buildings, still in use by the Garda Síochána. Over the centuries, the castle was the centre of the web of the security apparatus which kept Ireland under control. (See the film *Michael Collins* for depictions of espionage and derring-do within the castle.)

Enter the delightful wide and green park at the rear of the castle, a pleasant spot to take a rest. Constructed at the end of the 20th century, the swirling patterns are supposed to depict the eels of *Dubh Linn*, the black pool of the city's origins.

The Chester Beatty Library is at the western side of the park and very much deserves a visit (p.14).

Dubh Linn Gardens

Castle St, D2 ☎ *01 6458813*
www.dublincastle.ie
Tour times:
Mon–Sat 10am–4.45pm
Sun 12am – 4.45pm
Admission: €4.50

St Patrick's Hall

The Dublin Castle tour offers a chance to see the impressive rooms and decor of the State Apartments as well as a snapshot of the Irish historical experience. In the throne room, it is said that the legs of the throne had to be cut down to allow Queen Victoria to sit with decorum during her first visit to Ireland in 1849. Further on in the drawing room, one can see the portraits of the young queen and her consort, Prince Albert.

Portraits of the viceroys fill the picture gallery. The full pageantry of the viceregal era is evident in St Patrick's Hall. Lavish State Balls were held here. There are galleries at either end, used by musicians. The standards of the knights of the Order of St Patrick hang around the hall. The central ceiling painting is a magnificent piece of propaganda of its time (in the run-up to the Act of Union of the two kingdoms of 1801): it depicts George III seated between Britannia and Hibernia.

03 Chester Beatty Library

This is one of Dublin's treasure troves, a veritable gem of a museum and one of the best in Europe. The Chester Beatty Library has been described as the finest collection of manuscripts and books made by a private collector in the 20th century. Here are delightful artefacts representing the world's written heritage (artistic, religious and secular) from about 2,700 BC. It was designated European Museum of the Year in 2002.

It is divided into three collections: Western, Islamic and East Asian. There are Egyptian papyri and a host of oriental exhibits including Japanese prints and Chinese imperial jade books in the Emperor's own hand. There are exquisitely illuminated copies of Bibles and European Medieval and Renaissance manuscripts. The *Arts of the Book* include items such as the Chester Beatty Love Poems from Egypt of around 1160 BC. The Greek New Testament papyri are worth a visit in their own right.

The library is particularly strong in its exhibits of Islamic art. The collection of more than 250 Qur'ans is second only to the imperial collection in Istanbul. There are exhibitions of Turkish and Persian miniatures, in all their delicacy.

The library is housed in the 18th-century Clock Tower building, at the rear of the Dublin Castle grounds, which was the ordnance office of the Royal Engineers during the 19th century. It was sensitively refurbished and extended and now houses the collections.

The library is a hive of cultural activity. Special exhibitions, with highlights from the collections, are regularly presented. Watch out for the public tours on Wednesdays at 1pm and Sundays at 3 and 4pm, as well as a myriad of public lectures and films

throughout the week.

There is a fine glazed concourse area, which is an excellent place to pause and relax. Off this are a bookshop and the aptly named and excellent Silk Road Café with a menu from places like Afghanistan, Palestine and Greece. It is possible to go to the top floor for the Roof Garden which affords a panoramic view of the *Dubh Linn* Gardens in the Dublin Castle grounds.

Dublin Castle, D2 ☎*01 4070750*

www.cbl.ie

Opening times:

Mon-Fri 10am-5pm. Closed Mon Oct-April

Sat 11am-5pm; Sun 1-5pm

Admission: Free

Getting there: To the rear of Dublin Castle, by the *Dubh Linn* Gardens. A two-minute walk from Dame St (via the Palace St Gate of the castle) and close to Christ Church Cathedral (entrance via the Ship St Gate of the Castle).

Bus: 16, 123

Sir Alfred Chester Beatty, who left this library in trust for the public benefit, was very generous to Ireland.

Born in 1875 in New York, he studied engineering and became prominent as a mining consultant in the United States. He made his fortune from the development of the Copperbelt in Northern Rhodesia (now Zambia).

This avid collector gathered European and Persian manuscripts and later Qur'ans as well as oriental art. He settled in Dublin in 1950. He built a library in the south of the city to house his collection which opened in 1954. This was relocated to the present location in Dublin Castle in 2000. Beatty was made Ireland's first honorary citizen in 1957. When he died in 1968 he was given a unique accolade for a private citizen, a state funeral.

St Patrick's Cathedral

See two medieval Cathedrals, and one in waiting, all a legacy of Ireland's complex religious history. At the time of the Reformation, Dublin had two cathedrals, Christ Church and St Patrick's, which became part of the state church of the time, and thus are still part of the Anglican Communion (Church of Ireland). Remember that all mentioned here are functioning churches, services may be in progress, and due respect should be shown when visiting.

St Patrick's Cathedral is the second of Dublin's medieval cathedrals, founded in 1191. It is said that a sacred well in the park adjacent to the cathedral was where St Patrick, patron saint of Ireland, baptised converts around 450. There was much construction over the medieval years, but it was in a derelict state by the 19th century. The proceeds of the demon drink came to the rescue (as it had for similar work on Christ Church). Sir Benjamin Lee Guinness, of that family, funded an extensive reconstruction in Gothic style. A statue by the cathedral entrance commemorates him.

Enter the cathedral, and appreciate this perfectly preserved part of ecclesiastical life. Within are the graves of Jonathan Swift (writer, satirist and Dean of the cathedral 1713-1743) and his inamorata, Stella. Individual monuments commemorate various Irishmen who fought in the battles during Queen Victoria's reign including the Indian Mutiny, Crimean War, the Boer War and many 19th-century battles now faded into distant history.

St Patrick's Close, D8
☎ *01 4539472*
www.stpatrickscathedral.ie
Opening times:
Mon-Sat 9am-5pm
Sun check website
Admission: €5.50

Christ Church Cathedral was founded around 1030 by Sitric, king of the Dublin Vikings. However, the oldest extant remains here were built by the Anglo-Normans around 1186-1200. Much building was carried out in the centuries which followed. In 1395 King Richard II sat here to receive the homage of the native Irish kings. In 1487, during the reign of Henry VII, Lambert Simnel, the boy pretender to the English throne, was 'crowned' here as Edward VI.

In the 16th century, Henry VIII broke from Rome and the

cathedral came under the new direction. It changed briefly when James II attended Mass here in 1689 before his defeat at the Battle of the Boyne. The victorious William of Orange paid a visit after the battle in July 1690. He thanked God for his victory and donated gilt plate, now on display in the crypt.

The cathedral choir took part in the first performance of Handel's *Messiah* in 1742.

In the 1870s a whiskey distiller, Henry Roe, paid for a complete restoration of the cathedral.

Note the reconstructed tomb of Strongbow (the pre-eminent Norman conqueror). The *Treasures of Christ Church Exhibition* is located in the 12th-century crypt. As well as a presentation on the cathedral's history, there is a display of manuscripts and other artefacts.

Christ Church Cathedral

Christchurch Place, D8
☎ *01 6778099*
www.cccdub.ie
Opening times:
Mon-Sat 9.30am-6pm
Sun: check website
Admission: €6

Pro-Cathedral

As the discriminatory Penal Laws faded away at the beginning of the 19th century, the Catholics built a Pro-Cathedral (a church temporarily serving as the cathedral of a diocese) in what is now a run-down part of the city. It is ironic that Dublin, predominantly Catholic, still has not a full Roman Catholic cathedral.

North of the Liffey, **St Mary's Pro-Cathedral** is about halfway up Marlborough St. This neo-classsical church, dating from 1825, is largely modelled on the church of St Philippe du Roule in Paris. Within the austere interior, statues commemorate members of the Catholic hierarchy. Not surprisingly, there are no memorials to those who fought in imperial battles. The statue of Cardinal Cullen (who died in 1878) captures Cullen's aloof stature and is by Sir Thomas Farrell. Cullen directed the 19th-century Irish Catholic Church towards strict obedience to Rome. He diligently led the Church towards achieving a dominant position in Ireland – a position that has declined somewhat over recent decades.

05 Marsh's Library

Marsh's Library is called a treasury of the European mind. Come here to savour the experience of how Dublin was three centuries ago. Tucked away at the south side of St Patrick's Cathedral, it is a perfect example of a 17th-century scholar's library. This haven of literature and culture was built in 1701, designed by Sir William Robinson, the architect of the Royal Hospital, Kilmainham (p.64).

Walk through the gate with its Gothic arch and up the steps. Enter and be greeted by helpful staff. Walk the corridors among the dark oak bookcases, each with a carved and lettered gable, crowned with a mitre. Here is an opportunity to see, in bound leather or even vellum, examples of Europe's great cultural heritage. There are four main collections, ranging from the 16th to the early 18th century. It covers all the knowledge of that time with over 25,000 books on medicine, law, science, travel, navigation, mathematics, music, surveying and classical literature.

Archbishop Marsh collected the learned books of his time, capturing the birth of new ideas and the rise of science. In 1705 he purchased the Bishop of Worcester's collection of 10,000 books, then regarded as the finest private library in England.

The first librarian, Dr Bouhéreau, was a Huguenot who had fled France in 1695. He left his collection to the library, part of which is now an important source for the study of Calvinism in 17th-century France. The collections are still shelved as they were allocated by Marsh and Bouhéreau.

In addition to printed books, there is a collection of about 300 manuscripts in the library including the *Lives of the Irish*

Saints in Latin, dating from about 1400.

Each year there is a new exhibition of books on a selected theme from the Library's collection. Be sure to observe silence, as this is truly a working library, not a form of museum. Scholars labour on the treasures within.

While it now has discreet CCTV, the library comes from an era pre-dating these modern devices. Originally, many of the books were chained. Each book had a small metal clasp attached to a chain which ran on a wooden rod attached to each shelf. In a gallery at the rear of the library, there are three elegant wired alcoves or 'cages'. Here a reader would be locked away, to peruse a book in secure solitude, with no danger of larceny!

St Patrick's Close, D8

☏ *01 4543511*

www.marshlibrary.ie

Opening times:

Mon, Weds-Fri 9.30am -1pm; 2pm-5pm

Sat 10am-1pm

Admission: €2.50

Getting there: About 50 metres along the street from the entrance to St Patrick's Cathedral.

Bus: 49, 49A, 54A (from Eden Quay); 77, 77A (from Trinity College)

The library was founded by **Narcissus Marsh**, Archbishop of Dublin (1638-1713). His name may have been unusual, as were those of his brothers – Epaphroditus and Onesiphorus. Born in Wiltshire in England, he was sent to Ireland as Provost of Trinity College Dublin in 1679. He rose through the ecclesiastical ranks and was appointed Archbishop of Dublin in 1694.

Dissatisfied with the arrangements for scholars in Trinity College, he paid for the establishment of this building, using his own funds. When founded, it was the first public library in Ireland. A man of great culture and learning, Marsh left all his books to it, but his great collection of oriental manuscripts was left to the Bodleian Library in Oxford.

Marsh was instrumental in arranging the printing of Bishop Bedell's translation of the Old Testament into Irish, two volumes of which are in the Library. Marsh died in 1713 and is buried near his library, in the adjacent grounds of St Patrick's Cathedral.

06 Natural History Museum ★★

The National Museum of Ireland – Natural History has an extensive collection of natural history set in a splendid 19th-century building.

The opening of the museum in 1857 coincided with a public lecture in Dublin by the explorer David Livingstone. The building is relatively plain outside, but inside lies a sumptuous interior.

The Victorians had a hunger for knowledge, science and new discoveries. The museum, popularly known as the 'Dead Zoo', is a perfect example of a Victorian institution. The exhibition style and the glass cabinets with dark wood are as they were150 years ago. Here are collections of stuffed animals, trays of preserved specimens (including a collection of insects gathered by Charles Darwin). On display are zoological exhibits from all over Ireland and around the world. Some of this rich variety of animals is now endangered or extinct.

Many exhibits were brought back by Victorian explorers. Many of these, some also members of the British army and navy of that time, were Irish. The museum holds a large amount of material from outside Ireland, a legacy of these keen Irish amateurs and scientists abroad. The white polar bear was donated by Sir Francis Leopold McClintock, an Irish polar explorer, who went on the mid-19th century expedition that searched for the missing Franklin North West Passage expedition.

On the ground floor is the Irish Room, devoted to the variety of animals found in Ireland. In pride of place is an 11,000-year-old giant Irish deer. Suspended above the gallery, an unusual but appropriate centrepiece, is a 20-metre-long whale skeleton. There is a new Discovery Zone and Reading Area in the museum.

Outside, take a peek through the railings to the right at the superb statue of Prince Albert, tucked away in the grounds of Leinster House. You can catch a glimpse of the allegorical figures representing art, manufacturing, science and agriculture at its base.

Irish Room

The exploration theme is continued by **T. H. Parke's** statue in front of the museum. Parke was an army surgeon who participated in H. M. Stanley's expedition across Central Africa to rescue Emin Pasha (1887-89). Parke is reputed to be the first European to see the Ruwenzori, or Mountains of the Moon.

A bronze plaque below the statue shows Parke sucking poison from an arrow-wound in the chest of an expedition member. Stanley (with cap) can be seen to the right.

After Parke died in 1893 his coffin was drawn on a gun carriage through Dublin's streets to Broadstone Station and then by train to his native Leitrim.

Merrion St, D2. ☏ *01 6777444*

www.museum.ie

Opening times:

Tues-Sat 10am-5pm

Sun 2-5pm. Closed Mon, (including public holidays)

Admission: Free

Getting there: From College Green walk down the south side of Trinity College along Nassau St, via Leinster St South, Clare St, turn right up Merrion Square West to Merrion St entrance.

National Gallery of Ireland

Left: 'The Taking of Christ' by Caravaggio; Right: 'The Liffey Swim' by Jack B. Yeats

Visit here to enjoy outstanding art in fine surroundings. The National Gallery of Ireland is medium-sized – but has an outstanding collection of Western European art. Within these walls are over 14,000 paintings, sculptures and other works of art. It includes all the major European schools of painting. There are fine examples of works by Velázquez, Vermeer, Gainsborough, Goya, Poussin, Van Gogh, Monet and Picasso. The library benefitted in 1987 from a gift of 17 outstanding old master paintings from Sir Alfred and Lady Beit. Pictures from their collection in Russborough House (p.119) had been stolen by the IRA only to be stolen again by a ruthless Dublin criminal known as 'The General'. (See the films *The General*, with Brendan Gleeson, by John Boorman and *Ordinary Decent Criminal,* with Kevin Spacey).

Some visitors to Dublin are probably not aware of the wealth of Irish art which can be seen in the gallery. Prominent examples are works by Barry, Lavery, Maclise, Osborne, Leech and Orpen. The Yeats family, principally the poet W. B. Yeats' painter brother, Jack B. Yeats, have a room to themselves. The gallery also houses the National Portrait Collection.

In pride of place is *The Taking of Christ,* painted in 1602 by the Italian baroque master Caravaggio, then at the height of his fame. Caravaggio was a skilful manipulator of

light and shade, as shown by this (in places) luminous painting of Christ being kissed by Judas. The painting disappeared for over 200 years and was thought to be lost or destroyed. It had hung unknown for years in the refectory of the Jesuit community in Dublin's Leeson St. It was identified in the early 1990s and, now restored, is on display at the gallery, on indefinite loan from the Jesuit Fathers.

The Millennium Wing is a most successful example of modern architecture: constructed in honey-coloured stone, it blends in well with the original buildings.

Merrion Square West, D2
☎ *01 6615133*
www.nationalgallery.ie
Opening times:
Mon-Sat 9.30am-5.30pm
Sun 12pm-5.30pm
Admission: Free
Getting there: From College Green walk down the south side of Trinity College along Nassau St, via Leinster St South to the Clare St entrance.

William Dargan

It all started with the wealthy contractor **William Dargan**, known as the 'Father of Irish Railways', who organised the Exhibition of Art and Industry on Leinster Lawn in 1853. His statue stands in front of the National Gallery. Upright and industrious, Dargan was Queen Victoria's favourite Irishman. He declined a knighthood which she offered after visiting the exhibition. The paintings on show at the 1853 exhibition encouraged the great and the good of Dublin, with Dargan in the forefront, to set up the National Gallery in 1864.

Another significant figure is the Dublin-born writer and playright **George Bernard Shaw** (1856-1950), who credited the gallery for having contributed to his early education in Ireland. One of the reasons for the present wealth of paintings within the gallery is that Shaw willed a third of his royalties to it. This will continue up to 2020, when the copyright expires. Appropriately, there is a statue of Shaw on display inside.

National Library & Museum ★★

Left: Reading Room, National Library; Right: National Museum

On Kildare St can be found a concentration of culture, heritage and learning. Two institutions, the National Museum and National Library, mirror each other across the forecourt of Leinster House, home of Ireland's parliament. Both buildings were designed by T. N. and T. M. Deane, and opened in 1890. These buildings present rather staid faces, but have fine interiors.

Wisdom and learning is the theme in the **National Library of Ireland**. In the entrance hall, there are stained-glass windows depicting men of knowledge down through the ages. The mosaic on the floor with '*Sapientia*' (knowledge) presents a suitable welcome.

The fine wooden carvings on the doors are are by Carlo Cambi of Siena, who also provided similar in the National Museum and the National Gallery. Deposit your bag and go up the staircase to look at the Reading Room. This D-shaped domed room, with its height, splendour and scholars researching at the old desks, is just the same as James Joyce experienced it at the beginning of the 20th century. The library has the world's most comprehensive collection of books on Ireland, manuscripts, and much else. Major exhibitions using material from the library are held. A free Genealogy Advisory Service is available for people who wish to trace their ancestors.

Kildare St, D1. ☎ *01 6030200*

www.nli.ie

Opening times:

Mon-Wed 9.30am-7.45pm; Thur-Fri 9.30am-4.45pm

Sat 9.30am-12.45pm

Admission: Free

Getting there: From College Green walk down the south side of Trinity College along Nassau St, turn right up Kildare St.

The National Museum of Ireland – Archaeology can be entered to the right of Leinster House. The entrance hall is a rotunda with a decorated cupola. Like its sister, the Library, across the way, it has a fine floor mosaic. When you enter the exhibition hall, pause and look at the ceiling – a wonderful array of Victorian cast iron.

Now turn to the exhibitions which range all the way back to 7000 BC. *The Treasury* shows outstanding examples of Celtic and medieval art. This includes the Ardagh Chalice, the Tara Brooch and the Derrynaflan Hoard. *Ór – Ireland's Gold,* displays the finest collection of prehistoric gold artefacts in Western Europe. *Prehistoric Ireland* presents the culture of prehistory. There are exhibits on the *Viking Ireland* and *Medieval Ireland 1150-1550.*

Kingship and Sacrifice centres on a number of Iron Age bog bodies. Look in particular at an electrifying exhibit of one such man. Human vanity was not invented recently: he was of high status, and his hair is in a quiff with a dash of resin.

Gold Torc

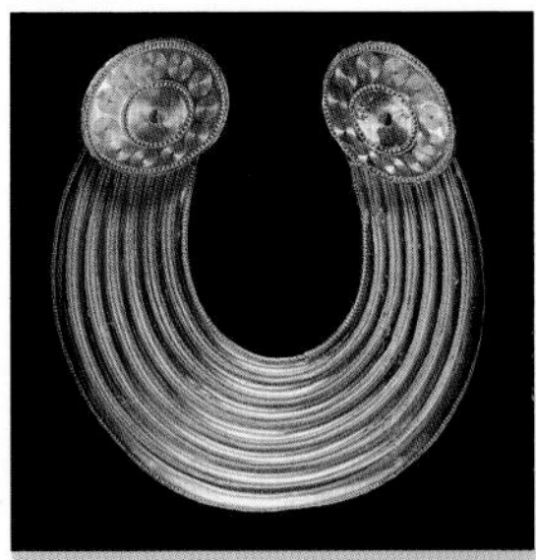

Kildare St, D1. ☎ *01 6777444*

www.museum.ie

Opening times:

Tues-Sat 10am-5pm

Sun 2pm-5pm

Closed Mon (incl. public holidays)

Admission: Free

Monkeys at Kildare Street Club

At No 2-3 Kildare St, at the Nassau St end, *Discover Your National Library* is a permanent exhibition based on the National Library's treasures. This red-brick building (which is shared with the Alliance Française at No 1) was formerly the **Kildare Street Club** and is worth close inspection. It was designed by the architect Sir Thomas Deane (whose son and grandson later designed the National Library and National Museum) and Benjamin Woodward. (See reference to their design of the Museum Building in Trinity College on page 11). Deane and Woodward also designed the Natural History Museum in Oxford University. This talented duo brought their team of stone-carvers with them to the Kildare Street Club. The result is the wonderful carved-stone decoration on display, including a collection of fantastical animals at the bases of the columns around the building. Observe the monkeys playing billiards at the column base, to the right of the entrance to the Alliance Française. Was this a comment by the stone carvers on the leisured occupants of the club?

National Concert Hall

Dublin has had more than a passing acquaintance with great music. **George Frederich Handel** got the best gig. He visited Dublin in 1741-2 when Dublin was at the height of its glory. Besides the construction of fine squares and imposing public buildings, the arts were not neglected. Theatres and concert halls flourished. Dublin was then, after London, the second city. Handel's new oratorio, the *Messiah*, was first performed in this bright and prestigious city. The premiere was held in Neal's Musick Hall in Fishamble Street on 13 April 1742. This is long since demolished and a plaque is all that remains. Every April, it is commemorated here with a spirited open-air rendition.

Fast-forward 300 years and probably the best-known Dublin musicians are **U2.** Their formative moments were when they met while at Mount Temple School in Marino. The Clarence (on Wellington Quay) was purchased by Bono and the Edge, who restored this Art-Deco hotel. The Octagon Bar is an impressive place to pause and enjoy a drink. U2's earlier recordings were made at Windmill Lane (near Sir John Rogerson's Quay). Now no longer a studio, it has a facing wall, with graffiti sprayed on by countless fans.

Other Dublin musicians include **Phil Lynott** of Thin Lizzy (*Whiskey in the Jar; The Boys are Back in Town*) who has a cult following. His statue, with guitar, is on Harry St (off Grafton St), outside the Bruxelles pub. **Bob Geldof** is a Dubliner and his Boomtown Rats first played in the city. **Sinéad O'Connor** is also from Dublin. If you really want to see it, there is a plaque in the Bad Ass Café (in Temple Bar) where she once waited table. **Enya,** Bono and other musical celebrities live in the fashionable suburbs of Dalkey and Killiney. **Boyzone** are a Dublin band who were formed in 1993.

Big ticket shows and musicians usually appear at the **O2 Venue,** North Wall, D1, a converted railway warehouse, *www.theo2.ie.* The Celtic dance show *Riverdance* was premiered here in 1995. **Michael Flatley** danced in the original Eurovision performance, and staged the premiere of his show *Lord of the Dance* here in 1996.

For serious music, head to the **National Concert Hall**, Earlsfort Terrace, D2, *www.nch.ie.* Classical music is mainly on offer here, with a sprinkling of light music and occasionally Irish traditional music.

There are free concerts of contemporary and classical music at noon on Sundays at the Hugh Lane Gallery (p.40).

Comhaltas Ceoltoirí Éireann at 32 Belgrave Square, Monkstown, Co. Dublin, *www.comhaltas.ie*, is active in the preservation of Irish traditional music.

The Pipers' Club at 15 Henrietta St, D1, *www.pipers.ie*, is devoted to an instrument unique to Ireland, the uilleann pipes.

For rock and other genres, good venues include: **Whelan's**, Wexford St, D2, *www.whelanslive.com* – great range of music in this lively place: rock, alt country music and more; **Vicar Street**, Thomas St D8, *www.vicarstreet.ie* – rock concerts and performances; **Button Factory**, Curved St, Temple Bar, D2, *www.thebuttonfactory.ie* – mix of rock performers and bands; **The Grand Social**, near Ha'penny Bridge, D1, *www.thegrandsocial.ie* – all kinds, from rock to traditional.

Phil Lynott (1949-1986)

One of the best ways to experience traditional music is at a session in a pub. It is friendly, chatty, and convivial. Frequently others join in and jam with the musicians. Some of the best pubs are:

The Cobblestone, 77 King St North, Smithfield, D7, *www.cobblestonepub.ie*. The website modestly claims that it is 'home of the finest traditional music and the best pints of Guinness any man can find'. Sessions: Mon & Tues from 9pm; Wed-Sat from 7pm; Sun from 2pm.

O'Shea's Merchant, 12 Lower Bridge St, D8. ☎ *01 6793797*. See 'set dancing' here (danced to Irish music, in square sets of four couples, originally adapted from French quadrilles). Sessions every Mon, Tues & Wed, with free classes every Mon.

Hughes, 19 Chancery St, D7. ☎ *01 8726540*. Located near the Four Courts. The musicians start around 10pm.

Devitt's, 78 Lower Camden St, D2. ☎ *01 4753414*. This is as authentic as it comes, great musicians. Sessions: Thurs, Fri, Sat, after 9.30pm.

The Duke, 8-9 Duke St D2 (off Grafton St). ☎ *01 6799553*. Historic pub with traditional sessions after 9.30pm on Sun.

Literary Dublin I: Great Writers 

Oscar Wilde Statue, Merrion Square

Ireland, and Dublin in particular, has an enviable record in literature in the English language. Is it because when that language was imposed on the speakers of the native Irish language over the centuries, the Irish took the new English language and did it better? Whatever the reason, Ireland, a small country, has had four Nobel laureates in literature: George Bernard Shaw; William Butler Yeats; Samuel Beckett and, in 1995, Seamus Heaney – all of whom either came from Dublin or lived in the city.

An early Dublin writer was the Dean of St Patrick's Cathedral, **Jonathan Swift**. Born in Dublin in 1667, he was a satirist, poet and political pamphleteer as well as a clergyman. He wrote his masterpiece, *Gulliver's Travels,* in 1726. Swift's grave, near to that of his inamorata, Stella, can be seen in St Patrick's Cathedral (p.16).

In front of Trinity College on College Green, can be seen the statues of two Trinity contemporaries. **Oliver Goldsmith** (born 1730) wrote *The Vicar of Wakefield* and the play *She Stoops to Conquer* and is remembered for his poem *The Deserted Village*. **Edmund Burke** (born 1729) was a political writer and became the leading orator and theorist of the Whig party in London.

William Butler Yeats, born in 1865, is known as the greatest modern Anglo-Irish poet. The leader in the Irish Literary revival which led to the establishment of the Abbey Theatre, he lived at 82 Merrion Square in the 1920s. He died in 1939 and his epitaph, taken from one of his poems, is the masterly

Cast a cold Eye
On Life, on Death.
Horseman, pass by!

Samuel Beckett was born in the Dublin suburb of Foxrock in 1906. He eventually settled

Samuel Beckett

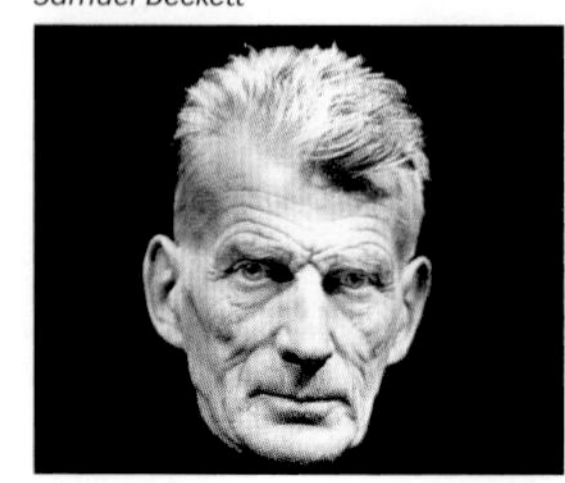

in Paris in 1937 and joined the Resistance there during the war. His spare, minimalist works include *Waiting for Godot* as well as others like *Endgame* and *Happy Days*. He was awarded the Nobel Prize in 1969. He is honoured in Dublin by the emblematic Samuel Beckett Bridge (p.97).

Oscar Fingal O'Flahertie Wills Wilde was born in Dublin in 1854. Trinity College was followed by Oxford University, where he cultivated his sense of aestheticism. In due course, he moved to London and was variously a journalist, critic and writer of poetry, prose and plays. His plays include *Lady Windermere's Fan*, *The Importance of Being Earnest*, and *An Ideal Husband*. He flew high in London society and fell to earth following trials in 1895 associated with his homosexuality. Two years' hard labour in Reading Gaol followed. He died in 1900.

For a short walk on the Wilde side, go to 21 Westland Row to see the plaque commemorating his birthplace. Walk to the corner of Clare St and Merrion Square North. At 1 Merrion Square is the handsome Victorian building where Wilde spent his formative years. Across the road at the corner of Merrion Square Park is a statue of Wilde, languidly reposing on a rock. Composed of marble and fine stone, it captures the spirit of this brilliant and witty aesthete.

Shaw Birthplace

George Bernard Shaw, born in Synge St in 1856, achieved fame with his plays *Arms and the Man*, *John Bull's Other Island*, *Major Barbara*, *St Joan* and *Man and Superman*. He was the only person who won a Nobel Prize (1925) and an Oscar (for his adaptation of his own play, *Pygmalion*, 1938). The National Gallery of Ireland benefits from a bequest from Shaw. Royalties from his *My Fair Lady* have funded many purchases of paintings.

The George Bernard Shaw Birthplace is worth a visit. This modest two-storey over basement terraced house dates from 1840. It is atmospheric and features portraits of Shaw, his family and scenes from his plays. His wit and idiosyncracy shine through in a letter where he specified the plaque to be erected outside this house could be in marble or plaster, but not metal. Here you can experience how it was to live in a Dublin Victorian home.

33 Synge St, D8
☎ *01 4750854*
Opening times: Jun-Aug
Tues, Thur, Sat 11am-3.30pm
Closed Sun
Admission: €6.00
Getting there: 10 minutes south-west from St Stephen's Green
Bus: 16, 16A, 19, 19A, 122

Literary Dublin II: James Joyce

Joyce (right) in Paris

James Joyce is considered Ireland's greatest modern writer. His masterpiece, *Ulysses*, is regarded as the outstanding twentieth-century novel.

Born in 1882 in Brighton Square, Rathgar, he had a peripatetic childhood: his father continuously moved house to put his creditors off his scent.

In 1904, Joyce went to Trieste, then in its glory days as the premier port of Austro-Hungary, where he spent his impecunious time teaching English. It was there that he commenced writing *Ulysses*. Joyce maintained an affection for Dublin. He was reputed to have been able to name all the shops in sequence up one side of (the long) Talbot Street and back down the other side.

His works include *Dubliners*, *Finnegans Wake* and *A Portrait of the Artist as a Young Man*. He died in Zurich in 1941. It is worth seeing *The Dead*, the last film by John Huston, (1987) based on his most famous short story, centred around a dinner set in 15 Usher's Quay, D8, on the south Liffey quays.

Appropriately, the adjacent Calatrava-designed James Joyce Bridge frames a vista of the house, as seen from the north side of the river.

The **James Joyce Centre** has exhibits on his life and works. On the top floor of this restored Georgian house, it is possible through interactive installations and three films, to delve into *Ulysses*, its historical backdrop, and learn more about Joyce's life. There are interesting items including a copy of Joyce's

Joyce statue, North Earl St

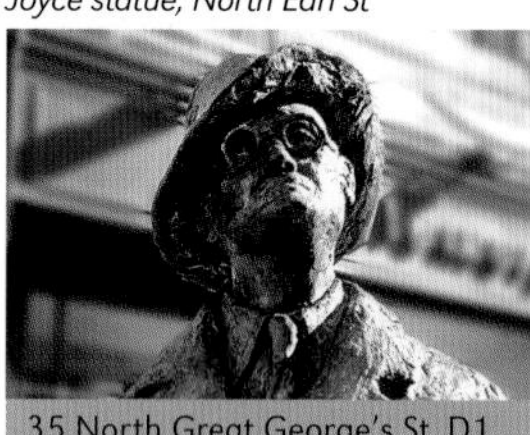

35 North Great George's St, D1
☎ *01 8788547*
www.jamesjoyce.ie

Joyce Centre opening times:
Mon-Sat 10am-5pm. Closed Mon, Oct-Mar
Sun 12am-5pm

Admission: €5

Getting there: From the top of O'Connell St, go east along Parnell St. Take first left.

death-mask. Downstairs, on display in a courtyard, can be seen the front door of No 7 Eccles St, Bloom's fictional home in *Ulysses*. The centre organises lectures and a Bloomsday Festival on 16 June as well as regular themed walking tours. These include: *A Joyce Circular*, *Dubliners* and *In the Footsteps of Leopold Bloom*. See website for details.

The **James Joyce Tower & Museum**, Sandycove, was originally one of a series of Martello towers built to defend against an invasion by Napoleon. It is the setting for the opening scene in *Ulysses*, where Stephen Dedalus views Dublin Bay, while Buck Mulligan shaves. Joyce stayed briefly in the tower in 1904. It is now a museum devoted to the life and works of Joyce. There are artefacts such as personal possessions of Joyce. On a fine day you can get an excellent view of the bay and mountains from the gun platform.

Joyce Tower

Sandycove Harbour, Sandycove
☎ *01 2809265*

Tower opening times: Apr-Aug
Tues-Sat 10am-1pm.; 2pm-5pm
Sun 2-6pm
Admission: €6.00
Getting there: Take the DART to Sandycove and Glasthule Station

Sweny's Pharmacy

Ulysses is the quintessential Dublin novel, being the wanderings around the city by one Leopold Bloom, advertising salesman, on 16 June 1904. Here are a few places you can try yourself:

Sweny's Pharmacy: This is in Lincoln Place, where, in *Ulysses*, Leopold Bloom purchased his soap of *sweet lemony wax*. If no longer a pharmacy, it is now an atmospheric place to visit, with lots of Joyce memorabilia. You can still buy the soap here, a great souvenir. Not far away, you can see the outline of the name Finn's Hotel on the gable of the redbrick building at Lincoln Place (at the end of the college railings) This is where Nora Barnacle (Joyce's wife) was working as a chambermaid when they first met, before eloping.

Davy Byrne's Pub, 21 Duke Street. A good place to take a break. *Moral pub. He doesn't chat. Stands a drink now and then. But in leap year once in four. Cashed a cheque for me once.* Here Bloom had a gorgonzola sandwich and a glass of red wine for lunch.

Literary Dublin III: Writers' Museum

Dublin Writers' Museum

This is literate and lively Dublin on display in a fine Georgian house. Dublin, one of the smallest of the great cities, has one of the finest literary traditions in the world, celebrated here. You can see displays on the leading writers and their works.

It includes Swift and Sheridan, Wilde and Shaw, Yeats, Joyce and Beckett. Not to be forgotten are other writers and playwrights like Seán O'Casey (*Juno and the Paycock*; *The Silver Tassie*) and Brendan Behan (*The Quare Fellow*; *The Hostage*). Literary Ireland rolls on and there are exhibits on contemporary Irish writers who continue the tradition, such as Seamus Heaney, Roddy Doyle, John Banville and Anne Enright.

On display are personal items, books, letters and portraits of writers. There is a note from George Bernard Shaw refusing to provide an autograph, and Brendan Behan's letter from the US observing that Broadway was a *great spot for a quiet piss-up*.

The Museum is housed in a restored Georgian building on Parnell Square. This was rebuilt comprehensively in the 1890s for George Jameson, of the whiskey-distilling family.

The building is worth looking at for its fine architectural detail, such as the elaborate Georgian plaster ceilings, particularly that in the Gallery of Writers on the first floor. The Victorian stained glass windows, installed by Jameson, can be seen by the staircase. There are pre-Raphaelite figures depicting the arts and science on the windows, with the Jameson family crest at the base of one of these. The museum has a good café and a bookshop. If you would like fine (but expensive) dining, the Michelin-starred Chapter One restaurant is next door.

Gallery of Writers

18 Parnell Square North, D1
☎ *01 8722077*
www.writersmuseum.ie
Opening times: Mon-Sat 10am-5pm; Sun 11am-5pm
Admission: €7.50
Getting there: Walk north from O'Connell St, along Parnell Square East, then turn left.

Figures in Dublinia

Here is a tableau of Viking and medieval Dublin, located in an impressive Victorian building.

Engage, learn and share says the brochure. Early Dublin is interpreted in a light-hearted way and you get an appreciation of how the city looked many centuries ago. It is set in the former Synod Hall of Christ Church Cathedral (p.16). This example of Gothic-Tudor revival architecture was built as part of the cathedral restoration works of the 1870s funded by the whiskey magnate Henry Roe.

The senses are exercised here, at least some of them (for sound, notably the farting man in the privy, and more pleasantly, the smell of spices at the medieval market). Unlike many museums, the visitor is encouraged to handle many of the exhibits, as well as waking up to 'smell the (medieval equivalent of) coffee'.

Dublin was founded by the Vikings and they get their due appreciation here. The ground floor has exhibits on Viking Dublin. Aspects of Viking life can be seen including a house, warriors and weapons. On the next floor, you can get a feel of how the medieval city was organised. The talking heads speak in an English accent – because Dublin was an English city for many centuries – hence there is an Irishtown in Dublin outside the walls! The first two floors succeed in bringing the history of the early city to life, albeit in a Disneyesque manner.

The third floor brings a change of pace. It is devoted to the excavations of the Viking settlements in the vicinity, with perhaps too much detail on the minutiae of archaeology.

Exit via the bridge over the road which leads to Christ Church Cathedral. As you walk along the bridge look at the wonderful timber roof and the stained-glass windows.

St Michael's Hill, D8
☎*01 6794611*
Opening times:
Apr-Sep daily 10am-5pm
Oct-Mar daily 10am-4.30pm
Admission: €7.50
Getting there: Next to Christ Church Cathedral
Bus: 49, 49A, 54A, 121, 123, 150

14 Dame Street Stroll

Tapestry, Battle of the Boyne

This is an agreeable ramble, with great Georgian architecture at each end and shades of Victorian Venetian fantasy in between. Start at the imposing Bank of Ireland on College Green. With Trinity College to your right, observe the imposing colonnaded piazza of the former Irish Parliament, now the bank. This was completed in 1739 to a design by Edward Lovett Pearce. Later additions were by James Gandon in 1785 (for his other works, see p.50).

This was the first purpose-built bicameral assembly building in Europe. This classical building, with its assertive grandeur, reflects the rich and confident place that Dublin had become in the 18th century. There were two houses: the Commons and the Lords. All came to an end when (following the 1798 Rebellion, and with not a few bribes) the Irish Parliament voted to join the parliament in London, under the Act of Union of 1801. It became a bank soon afterwards and the public banking hall was built in place of the House of Commons. However, the House of Lords is still intact and you can visit here (free tours from 11am, Tues). You can see the mace of the Irish House of Commons as well as the woolsack of the Lord Chancellor. Prominent are the two fine tapestries depicting the Siege of Derry and King William at the Battle of the Boyne.

Now walk west towards Dame St. On the south side you can see the exuberant façades of the banks which were built during the 19th century, in what was then the financial heart of the city. They brought a touch of exoticism to the dull world of banking. Above 34 College Green stands the statue of Erin, the personifaction of Ireland, flanked by a wolfhound, shamrocks and other national symbols. This started as the National Bank, founded by the great 19th-century nationalist politician Daniel O'Connell. At 27 College Green and the corner of Suffolk St, the bank (once the Hibernian Bank, now National Irish Bank) has wonderful stone carvings both inside and outside. The banking hall within has a perfect coffered plaster ceiling with a border of flowers and fruit. On the other side of the street, the Central Bank building, fronted by a busy plaza, casts a sombre shadow, as if a metaphor for a history of lax regulation in the Celtic Tiger era.

To lift your spirits – observe the exotic touch at the corner of Dame St and Fownes St, next to the plaza. Originally it was the Crown Life Office and is now a hotel and café. It was designed by Thomas Newenham Deane in 1868 with echoes of a Venetian palazzo.

Further west up Dame St, on the south side, is another bank in the north Italian style, again by Deane dating from 1874. This is the AIB at 7-12 Dame St, on the corner with Palace St. It is of rather dull limestone, but has decorative and carved stone inserts. In the banking hall within, the plasterwork details are particularly fine.

For more Victoriana, look across the road at the colourful stained-glass canopy of the Olympia theatre, once Dan Lowry's Music Hall. Complete the walk by visiting the City Hall, (see panel).

Clock, AIB

Mosaic in City Hall

The City Hall is situated at the Cork Hill entrance to Dublin Castle. Completed in 1779 (to designs by Thomas Cooley), it is one of Dublin's outstanding Georgian buildings. It forms the focus of the vista from Capel Street, along Essex Bridge and Parliament St. Originally the Royal Exchange, (a centre for merchants) it is now used by the City Council.

Enter the domed Round Hall with impressive marble statues set around. Many historic events took place here including the lying-in-state of the remains of Michael Collins, assassinated in 1922 during the Civil War. Look up at the murals around the dome, depicting the city's early history.

The *Story of the Capital* exhibition in the vaults can be entered via stairs or an elevator. This is a multimedia exhibition of how Dublin evolved. On display are many artefacts including the great Sword and Mace of Dublin, as well as the Lord Mayor's gold chain of office which was a gift from William of Orange in 1698.

Dame St, D2 ☏01 2222204
Opening times:
Mon-Sat 10am-5pm
Sun closed
Admission: exhibition €4

15

Merrion Square

Fitzwilliam Square, East to the left

The development of Georgian Dublin commenced north of the Liffey at the beginning of the 18th century and soon spread to the south of the river. Houses were built around Merrion Square from the 1760s onwards. The square was once private but is now a public park. On weekends the park railings become colourful as artists hang their paintings for sale around three sides of the perimeter. On Merrion Square West, cast your eyes on Leinster House, home of Ireland's Parliament (the *Dáil* is the lower house; the *Seanad* the upper house). This was designed for the Earl of Kildare by Richard Cassels and completed in 1747, with the objective of being the finest mansion in Dublin. The Irish architect, James Hoban, copied its façade when he designed the White House in Washington, completed in 1800.

Go into the park at the west side entrance. Inside you will see a small pyramid, a memorial to members of the Irish Defence Forces. Turn right and walk around the inner perimeter path. Statues that you encounter include a bust of Michael Collins, the lost hero of the Irish Civil War. For a touch of surrealism in the middle of the park, see the weird throne, the 'Joker's Chair', a memorial to Dermot Morgan, star of the irreverent *Father Ted* TV series.

The park is laid out in grassy lawns and colourful flower beds. Located around the park are various examples of old lamp standards used by Dublin Corporation, from the gas light era through to modern times. Roughly mid-way along the north perimeter path is a statue of Bernardo O'Higgins, the 19th-century liberator of Chile. On the north-west corner you find the fine statue of Oscar Wilde, observing his former home across the street in a languorous manner.

Exit the park by the south entrance. Turn left, due east along Merrion Square South.

The elegant Georgian houses are terraced, with a basement, and with granite steps leading to a fine entrance door. Large fanlights and windows allow natural light into the hall and rooms, at a time when artificial lighting was poor. Note the colourful doorways, a feature characteristic of Georgian Dublin. Doorscrapers are at each door, necessary when roads were muddy and full of horse-dung. On reaching the end of the street, look along Mount St Upper and enjoy one of the best vistas in Dublin, along the street which nobly terminates at St Stephen's Church, in Mount St Crescent. Known as the Peppercanister, the church was completed in 1824. This is the best neo-classical building in Ireland and features copies of parts of three ancient buildings in Athens.

Continue south along Fitzwilliam St Lower, past the modern offices of the ESB, an electricity utility. These were built in the1960s, thus altering a fine Georgian streetscape. Further along is Fitzwilliam Square. The square is a relatively quiet quarter of the city and gives a flavour of refined Georgian town living.

Vista along Mount St Upper

The Georgian House Museum, on the corner of Mount St and Fitzwilliam St, is a restored middle-class house of the late-18th century. It was painstakingly reconstructed by the ESB. Was this in reparation for its demolition of the Georgian streetscape of Fitzwilliam St decades before?

The Museum offers an opportunity to experience a Georgian house and get a glimpse of life as lived by a middle-class Georgian family and their servants. The tour is informative and wittily brings you back to the Georgian era in Dublin. You can see the servants' quarters in the basement, the fine public room at the next level and the plainer bedrooms upstairs. The museum contains period furniture from the National Museum collections. There is a café and a shop in the basement.

29 Fitzwilliam St Lower, D2
☎01 7026165

Opening times:

Tues-Sat 10am-5pm

Sun 12am-5pm

Admission: €6

Getting there: At the corner of Mount St Upper and Fitzwilliam St Lower

16 St Stephen's Green

Left: Iveagh Gardens; Right: St Stephen's Green

Once a marshy common, St Stephen's Green was enclosed in 1663. There is a grim historical association: the west side once boasted a gallows.

Fine houses were built around the park in the latter part of the 18th century. The green was landscaped in its present shape by the philanthropic Lord Ardilaun (of the Guinness family) in 1880. The Royal College of Surgeons had objected to the landscaping of the green. The good lord chose to site his statue on the perimeter facing the college.

The park bustles with people, yet affords a pleasant place to stroll in the heart of the city. Ramble along the tree-lined walks, past the colourful flowerbeds. There is an ornamental lake with the usual ducks and other birds (great for children, who enjoy feeding them). Bands give concerts at the bandstands during the summer.

There are many statues, including those of Yeats and Joyce. Located centrally is one of Countess Markiewicz, who, despite her aristocratic background, was a fervent revolutionary in Ireland's fight for freedom. It is appropriate that she be commemorated here as she fought in the Irish Citizen Army detachment in the adjacent Royal College of Surgeons during the 1916 Rising. The memorial to Wolfe Tone (father of Irish Republicanism) on the north-east corner, with its gaunt figure of Tone and flanked by upright stone slabs, is eye-catching. It has been dubbed 'Tonehenge'.

Exit the park on the southwest corner and turn left along St Stephen's Green South. The red-brick University Church, with its beautifully carved entrance is at 87A (see panel). Nearby at 85-86 is Newman House, with some of the best Georgian plasterwork in the city.

Further east at 79-81 are the classical porticos of Iveagh House, once the townhouse of Lord Iveagh of the Guinness family (brother of Lord Ardilaun). The house was donated to the Irish State in 1939 and is now the Department of Foreign Affairs.

Continue along to the end of the street, turn right at the corner and head down Earlsfort Terrace. The classical façade of the National Concert Hall is seen on the right. Previously home to University College Dublin, the Concert Hall was established in 1981 and now hosts a range of events from classical concerts to light entertainment. The original building, parts of which remain, hosted the 1865 Dublin Exhibition. The façade dates from 1914. The great cast-iron hands on the gate uprights date from 1872. Turn the corner and walk west along Hatch St Upper. Halfway along turn right and enter a discreet gate which leads into one of Dublin's hidden gems, the Iveagh Gardens. This park is one of the best places to escape the city hubbub. It was once owned by the Guinness family and is now a public park. There are sunny glades, a rustic grotto and archery grounds. Fountains and classical statues can be seen at the centre of the great lawns. In the north-east corner, there is a life-size statue of the great Irish tenor, John McCormack, singing his heart out.

John McCormack

University Church

Most 19th-century Dublin churches are of the classical or Gothic style. **The University Church**, 87A St Stephen's Green South, presents a refreshing change. The compact red-brick frontage to the street is a harbinger of the Byzantine style within. It has similarities to a church in Rome, S. Paolo fuori le Mura. Designed by John Hungerford Pollen, it was built to the requirements of the English convert to Catholicism, John Henry Newman (later a Cardinal) in 1856. He set up the Catholic University of Ireland, based next door in (what is now, the appropriately named) Newman House. There is a bust of Newman in the church. The design was influenced by the Victorian art critic John Ruskin's *Stones of Venice*. Richly ornamented, it succeeds in creating a large and airy space devoted to heavenly matters. The eminent architectural historian, Maurice Craig, called it *a delightful building ... emphatically re-vival rather than sur-vival.*

17 Hugh Lane Gallery

Come here to see a major collection of modern art, with a tragic story attached to it, set in an Earl's magnificent townhouse. The Dublin City Gallery, the Hugh Lane, is home to outstanding Irish and continental paintings.

The core of its collection, that of Sir Hugh Lane, arrived here long after a famous disaster. Sir Hugh was born in County Cork in 1875, and was brought up in Britain. He began a career as an art restorer and in time became a wealthy London art dealer. He developed an interest in Irish art and began a campaign to establish a gallery of modern art in Dublin. In a signed (but unwitnessed) codicil to his will he left his outstanding collection of Impressionist paintings to Dublin. Sadly, Sir Hugh drowned on the liner *Lusitania* which was torpedoed and sank in 1915, off his native county, Cork. The bequest was subsequently disputed by the National Gallery in London and a right royal battle broke out over custody. A compromise was reached only in 1959 and the bequest is now rotated between Dublin and London.

The collection has now grown to over 2,000 works of art. As well as works by prominent Irish and international painters there

Paintings by left, Osborne and right, Monet.

are those of the Impressionists including Monet, Manet, Degas, and Renoir. The gallery also hosts visiting exhibitions of contemporary art.

The gallery is located in what was the town house of James Caulfield, Earl of Charlemont. Construction started in 1763, to a design by Sir William Chambers (who also designed the impressive Somerset House in London). Chambers also designed the Casino at Marino (p.76) for Charlemont. The gallery building, sensitively restored, affords an opportunity to imagine how a grand aristocrat lived in Georgian Dublin.

Breton Girl, by Roderick O'Conor

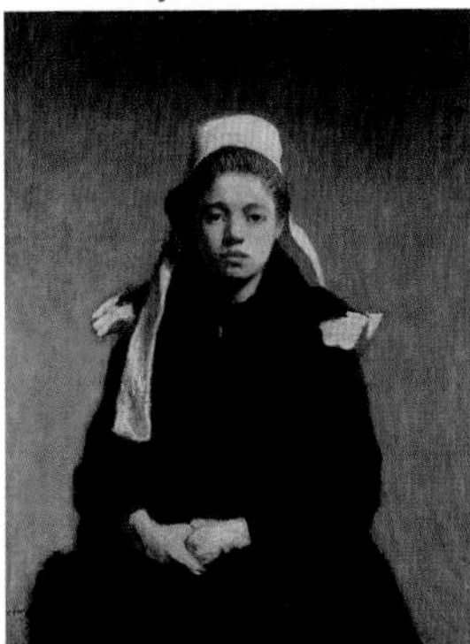

Parnell Square North, D1
☎ *01 2225550*
www.hughlane.ie
Opening times:
Tues-Thurs 10am-6pm
Fri-Sat 10am-5pm; Sun 11am-5pm
Admission: Free
Getting there: Walk north from O'Connell St, along Parnell Square East, then turn left.

Francis Bacon's Studio

In the Hugh Lane Gallery there is an added bonus: the opportunity to see a studio where a frenetic genius, now highly regarded, once worked.

Francis Bacon was born at 63 Lower Baggot St in Dublin in 1909. After experiencing Paris and louche Weimar Berlin in his early years, he eventually moved to London, where he spent the rest of his life.

Bacon died in 1992 and his heir donated the contents of his studio to the gallery. The studio, at 7 Reece Mews in London, was dismantled and relocated to Dublin in 1998 where it was painstakingly reconstructed. It includes the original doors, walls, floors and ceilings. There are slashed canvases, books, magazines and drawings.

Ingeniously presented, you can look in from several vantage points. You can see the almost dissolute clutter of this artist's studio. Despite this, or more likely because of this, Bacon turned out great works of art. It provides a unique insight into the idiosyncratic way he produced his paintings.

Left: Grand Chapter Room; Right: Royal College of Physicians

Make an appointment to see some exceptional Dublin buildings, all close to each other.

The **Freemasons' Hall** is one of Victorian Dublin's hidden delights. It is home of the Grand Lodge of Ireland, which dates from 1725, the second oldest in the world.

The present building opened in 1869, and includes lodge rooms, a library, and a museum. The lodge rooms are in a fantastical style: the Prince Masons and the Preceptory have medieval and knightly themes; the Grand Lodge Room is the size of a small parliament and is elaborately decorated. The Grand Chapter room is in Egyptian style with two sphinxes guarding it. Conducted tours can be arranged (with 24 hours' notice). ☎ *01 6761337*. 17 Molesworth St, D2.

The **Royal College of Physicians of Ireland**, founded in 1654, is the oldest surviving medical institution in the country. The RCPI building was constructed in 1864. Inside are several grandly appointed halls, with outstanding decoration. On display are busts of eminent physicians. The Heritage Centre has a collection of paintings, artefacts and books on the history of medicine in Ireland.

For a tour of the building contact heritagecentre@rcpi.ie or ☎ *01 6698801*. 6 Kildare St, D2.

The **Royal Irish Academy** is an independent academic body that promotes study in the sciences, humanities and social sciences. Established in 1785, it was granted a Royal Charter in 1786. The Academy Library holds the largest collection of historical Irish manuscripts in the world. It is an important research centre for Irish studies. It is located in a Georgian building. The former library, now the Meeting Room, added around 1852, is one of the finest Victorian meeting places in Dublin. Some furnishings come from the old Irish Parliament in College Green. The library is open Mon-Thurs 10am-5.30pm; Fri 10am-5pm. Group visits by appointment. ☎ *01 6762570*. 19 Dawson St, D2.

Royal Irish Academy

Left, Temple Bar Pub; Right, National Photographic Archive

This is an old part of Dublin, upgraded as the Celtic Tiger was learning to roar. A mixture of cobbled streets, high culture and a clutter of pubs, it is worth having a wander around. Caution: be careful here in the dark, when the bacchanalian effects of too much alcohol can be seen.

The name Temple Bar comes from Sir John Temple, who, in 1656 purchased a patch of waste ground between the river and Dame Street. Over the next century the area was laid out with music halls, residences and craftsmen's premises, such as those of printers and instrument-makers.

By the mid-20th century it was a run-down area and the national transport company started buying up properties with a view to developing a bus station. In the interim, shops were leased out at short-term low rents. The area developed a Left Bank culture, with a youthful and alternative atmosphere. In 1990 the Government decided to develop the area. Since then large investments have been made towards creating a cultural, commercial and residential quarter.

Here are narrow cobbled and pedestrianised streets, art centres, shops, restaurants and pubs. There is a remarkable array of shops aimed at a younger audience: clothes; jewellery; record shops. To the west, Cow's Lane has shops of a high-class nature. There are several outdoor markets in the area, including the Cow's Lane Fashion and Design Market every Saturday.

Temple Bar has served as a laboratory for new Irish architecture. Meeting House Square is interesting, particularly the hinged proscenium arch to the Ark cultural centre for children.

Arts centres abound and include the Irish Film Institute, 6 Eustace St, *www.ifi.ie* and the Project Arts Centre 39 East Essex St, *www. projectartscentre. ie.* In Meeting House Square is the National Photographic Archive, *www.nli.ie* and the Gallery of Photography, *www. galleryofphotography.ie,* both with free exhibitions.

20 Guinness Storehouse

The entrance to the Guinness brewery at St James's Gate in Dublin is a historic location. This was where pilgrims used to gather at the start of a pilgrimage to Compostela in Spain (said to be where St James is buried). Tourists gather here nowadays to see where Arthur Guinness founded his brewery in the 18th century. The brewery has been modernised and ownership has moved abroad. A staggering three million pints of Guinness are produced daily in this, the biggest stout export brewery in the world.

The Market Street Store was built in 1904 as a fermentation house. It was the first steel-framed building in Britain or Ireland to be built in what was called the Chicago style, with steel girders forming the main structure of the building, and the brick walls as infill panels. It has been expensively refurbished as a visitor centre, the Guinness Storehouse. The display has everything you might want to know about Guinness, its history and how it is made.

It is a buzzing, lively place with lifts available to whisk you to its many floors. Well designed, every effort is made to involve the visitor. There are cafés and restaurants, recipes

Barrels in cooperage display

on cooking with Guinness, as well as instruction on the craft of pouring a perfect pint. (One was poured for a bemused Queen Elizabeth II during her visit here in 2011).

Through the windows you can occasionally see the steam rising from the adjacent brewery, as it toils to make the black brew for the world.

Enjoy sipping your complimentary pint of Guinness at the top of the building in the Gravity Bar, a glass-fronted circular room with a panoramic view of Dublin. Some of the near surroundings are a bit pedestrian but you can cast your eyes to enjoy Dublin's finer buildings in the middle distance, and see the far-off Dublin bay and mountains.

Gravity Bar

St James's Gate, D8
☎01 4084800
www.guinness-storehouse.com
Opening times:
Daily 9.30am-5pm
(Jul-Aug 9.30am-7pm)
Admission: €15
Getting there: From Dame St walk straight ahead. Passing Christ Church continue onto Thomas St. At Crane St turn left, and at the end turn right onto Market St.
Bus: 51B, 78A from Aston Quay. 123 from O'Connell St/Dame St

Arthur Guinness was born in County Kildare in 1725. He set up a brewery in Leixlip and in 1759 moved to Dublin where he acquired a 9,000 years' lease on a premises at St James's Gate. The business grew, and in 1799 he decided to concentrate on the black brew (called porter, popular with porters in Covent Garden in London).

The coming of the railway and the steamship during the 19th century made it easy to transport the beer far and wide. The Guinness brewery expanded because of its ability to produce a high-quality product in a highly mechanised manner.

By 1886 the Guinness brewery was the biggest in the world and a generous employer to the large workforce. A narrow-gauge railway was used to transport barrels through the sprawling 50-acre complex to the adjacent Liffey whence they were carried by steam barges (with collapsible smoke stacks to get under bridges) to large steamers at the docks. Nowadays, the plant is highly automated, and the beer is more prosaically shipped for export using road tankers.

21 Old Jameson Distillery

In this old whiskey distillery, now a museum, you can discover how this smooth golden spirit is produced.

John Jameson's Distillery, constructed at Bow St in Smithfield in 1780, was one of the largest and finest in the world. It extended over two blocks with a multitude of buildings including grain stores, maltings, kilns, pot-still houses and cooperages. The boilerhouse chimney, dating from 1895, dominates the rather run-down square at Smithfield. The Jameson family was a prominent one. George Jameson had a fine Georgian house at 18 Parnell Square North, which he reconstructed. (Now the Writers' Museum, p.32). Another member of the family, Annie Jameson, was the mother of the inventor of radio, Guglielmo Marconi.

Nowadays the distilling of Jameson whiskey is carried out at Middleton, County Cork. Nevertheless, the one-hour tour (every 20 minutes) gives an opportunity to see how the traditional ingredients of water, barley and yeast, are transformed into whiskey. It starts off with an audio-visual presentation, followed by a guided walk through the recreated distillery. There are stills, barrels and all the things necessary to produce this precious liquid. It takes you through the seven stages of whiskey-making – from malting

and milling right through to triple distilling and maturation.

As the tour ends there is a complimentary glass of Jameson or a soft drink. At the end of the tour you have a chance to check out the premise – whether Irish whiskey really is the best. Volunteers are selected to participate in a tutored whiskey comparison (through taste, nose and finish) of Jameson Irish whiskey and premium Scotch and Bourbon whiskies.

Bow St, Smithfield, D7.
☎ *01 8072348*
www. jamesonwhiskey.com
Opening times:
Mon-Sat 9am-6pm
Sun 10am-6pm
Admission: €13.00
Getting there: Walk west along the quays to Inns Quay. After the Four Courts, turn right up Church St past St Michan's Church and then take the next left onto May Lane/Bow St.
Bus: 68, 69 & 79 from Aston Quay, 90 from Connolly & Heuston Stations. **Luas:** Red Line to Smithfield stop, three minutes' walk to the former Distillery.

Centuries ago, whiskey was the popular beverage of the masses. To cater for this, there was an extensive distilling industry in Dublin – 25 distilleries in 1800. The more efficient patent-still method was invented in 1830 by the Dubliner Aeneas Coffey and this was embraced by many distilleries in Scotland and those in the north of Ireland. Nevertheless, Dublin distilleries continued with the traditional pot-still method, believing that it produced a finer whiskey. (Note the spelling: whiskey, with an 'e' for the Irish variety. In Scotland, they call their product 'whisky'.) Around the end of the 19th century, Irish whiskey's reputation was the finest in the world. It was knocked off its perch when, after prohibition ended in 1933, the American palate had acquired a taste for bootlegged Scotch whisky. In recent decades, Irish whiskey has regained its international status as a sophisticated and fine-tasting spirit.

22 Museum, Collins Barracks

The **National Museum of Ireland – Decorative Arts and History** is housed in a former army barracks.

On an elevated position above the Liffey, this was once the Royal, then Collins, Barracks. Started in 1701, it was the largest public building constructed during King William III's reign, as well as being the first and grandest example of a large-scale residential barracks in Europe. In 1998 the buildings surrounding the main square were converted for museum use. The complex offers the opportunity to see an 18th-century military barracks and inspect the large square where generations of soldiers paraded. Military barracks have generally a spare and minimal aspect, as demonstrated here within its grey stone walls.

The museum includes fine examples of glassware, clothing, jewellery, furniture, folklife, coins and weaponry. The *Alfred Bender collection of Asian Art* is a recent addition. In the *Curator's Choice* section, amongst other treasures, there is a Japanese ceremonial bell, over 2000 years old.

Major collections include *Irish Silver, The Way We Wore: 250 Years of Irish Clothing and Jewellery* and *A Thousand Years of Irish Coins and Currency*.

The Easter Rising: Understanding 1916 offers an insight, albeit a little over-wordy, into this pivotal event in modern Irish history. Along the corridors you can see a marvellous example of performance art, a video, *100 Paces,* showing Irish soldiers marching, singing and drilling on the barracks square in a balletic whirl.

In the grounds to the west, you see the former quarters of the soldiers, and the cavalry stables, now converted for other uses.

It is worth exploring the area at the back. Walk north through the back gate and cross the

road at Arbour Hill. In front of you are the forbidding lines of a prison. It was once a military prison and dates from 1848. To the right is a church of 1850, in the Norman style, originally the prison chapel. To the right of this you can enter the grounds of the churchyard, once a military cemetery. Gravestones of Victorian soldiers are erected against the east wall.

At the northern end of the grounds is one of the pantheons of Irish nationalism. In a rather bleak and minimalist plaza lie 14 of the executed leaders of the insurrection of 1916. Among those buried in this location, after execution in Kilmainham Gaol, are James Connolly and Patrick Pearse. State ceremonies are regularly held here to commemorate the 1916 dead.

Gravestones, Arbour Hill

Benburb St, D7 ☏ *01 6777444*

www.museum.ie

Museum opening times:

Tues-Sat 10am-5pm

Sun 2-5pm Closed Mon (incl public holidays).

Admission: Free

Getting there: On the north side of the Liffey, near Wolfe Tone Quay.

Luas: The Red Line Museum stop is directly by the pedestrian entrance. **Bus:** 90, 25, 25A, 66, 67.

In pride of place at Collins Barracks is the exhibition entitled *Soldiers and Chiefs, the Irish at Home and Abroad 1550-2001*. Truly world-class, it is an opportunity to see the extraordinary role that Ireland has played in military matters over the centuries. This exhibition tells the story of Irishmen who served in foreign armies from the days of the Gallowglass mercenaries in the 16th century onwards. Numerous Irishmen were in the French and Spanish armies over the following centuries. There were liberators of Latin America from Bernardo O'Higgins of Chile to Admiral Brown who founded the Argentinean Navy. The participation by the Irish in the American Civil War is explored. During the centuries of occupation by Britain, Ireland was a source of recruits for the British forces. There are many details here of the Irish regiments in that service.

The exploits of the Irish Defence Forces are well displayed. Included is a 1950s Vampire jet fighter, an armoured car, as well as details of neutral Ireland's remarkable record in United Nations peace-keeping operations.

23 Gandon on the Liffey

Left: Custom House; Right: detail of lion, harp, unicorn and crown

This is a pleasant walk by the Liffey, where you see outstanding Georgian public buildings, designed by a brilliant 18th-century architect.

Start with the **Custom House** which is east beyond Eden Quay on the north quays. It is located just beyond the adjacent ugly Victorian railway bridge. (See panel for an optional stroll to the CHQ).

The young architect, James Gandon, living in London, had been invited to the Russian Court in St Petersburg in 1779. It was Dublin's fortune that he chose to come to the Irish capital instead, and began the design of the Custom House. It was a hugely expensive project – the cost amounted to one quarter of a year's revenue for the Irish Government. Construction began in 1781 in an excellent location. The quayside was a busy place with ships discharging cargo and it was convenient for the collection of customs duty.

The Customs House presents its finer façade to the quayside and is arguably Dublin's finest Georgian building. Here you can see the classical frontage, extending over 100m and clad in Portland stone. Allegorical sculptures on high include Commerce, Mercury, Neptune, Plenty and Industry. The keystones have heads representing Irish rivers. Those on the south face are (l. to r.): Foyle, Erne, Liffey, Boyne, Barrow/Nore. The Custom House was attacked in 1921 during the War of Independence. It burnt down and it took seven years to rebuild. The building now houses the Department of the Environment, but with the rather unenvironmentally-friendly example of the civil servants' cars parked around the sides of this classical building.

Face west and retrace your steps, on the north quays, along the Liffey. Cross O'Connell St and continue up river: four bridges (and one km) later you arrive at the **Four Courts**, where most of Ireland's highest courts are located. This was completed in 1802 to a design by Gandon. The neo-classical building exudes a feeling of power, and it is appropriate that it is at the

Four Courts

centre of the Irish legal system. In grey granite, it has an assertive drum and dome which dominate the skyline. On high, you can see the allegorical figures which include Justice, Mercy and Wisdom.

If you enter the building you may see, in the rotunda under the dome, the medieval spectacle of very important people dressed in black gowns, some wearing wigs – these are the barristers (lawyers entitled to appear in court). The ones in leisure wear may be the defendants. On occasion you may be lucky enough to see a black-robed judge pass through the hall, with a tipstaff (an assistant, with a staff tipped in silver) clearing their path.

This building also suffered in Ireland's turbulent early 20th century. In 1922 it was occupied by anti-Treaty forces during the Irish Civil War (which first erupted here over the acceptance of the Treaty signed with Britain). In what was the opening battle of the war, it was bombarded by the pro-Treaty side, which resulted in the eventual surrender of those within. The building was largely destroyed and was reconstructed in subsequent years. The shelling sequence was recreated for the film *Michael Collins.*

CHQ Building

If you feel like an additional excursion at the start of the walk, continue east from the Custom House, down North Wall Quay to the Irish Financial Services Centre. This once run-down docklands area was rehabilitated from the 1980s onwards, driven by tax incentives. There is now a mix of medium-rise offices and several squares with shops and restaurants serving the area.

A focal point of the area is George's Dock, dating from 1821. The docks here were eclipsed by the advent of the steamship. They proved too small and shipping moved to the deeper quays further east.

The adjacent **Custom House Quay** (CHQ) building is worth a look. Now a shopping mall, it has been sensitively restored. Originally a tobacco warehouse dating from around 1820, it has an impressive colonnade, still with the original cast-iron roof truss. With the largest clear floor area available in Dublin, it was chosen as the location for a banquet in 1856 given to welcome the Irish regiments home from the Crimean War.

Left: the GPO; Right: James Connolly statue

The 1916 Rising in Dublin, was a momentous event which led to Ireland's independence a few years later.

We begin with a view of the opposing side, namely a plaque to a fallen member of the British forces. Enter Trinity College, continue to the Berkeley Library and walk down the east side of the library buildings, along the edge of College Park, towards the boundary wall. Just to the left of a staircase leading to Nassau St is a plaque commemorating Private Smith, of the Fourth Hussars, killed during the rising. Trinity was defended against the rebels by the (loyalist) student Officer Training Corps.

Exit through Front Gate, turn right down Pearse St and walk to No 27. Now the Ireland Institute, it was once the Pearse family home. Patrick Pearse, educationalist, writer and revolutionary, was born here in 1879. He was involved in the setting up of the Irish Volunteers, was commander during the rising and signed the unconditional surrender. He was subsequently court-martialled and executed. A plaque commemorates Patrick and his brother Willie, a talented sculptor and painter, who also took part in the rising. Although not a leader, Willie was also executed, because he was Patrick's brother.

Plaque, Trinity College

Retrace your steps along Pearse St, turn right along Tara St and cross Butt Bridge. Opposite is Liberty Hall. This unprepossessing building, Dublin's tallest, was built in the 1960s to replace the original HQ of the Irish Transport and General Workers' Union, which was demolished by British artillery during the rising. James Connolly, leader of the union, had founded the Irish Citizen Army (ICA), the world's first ever socialist militia, in 1913. The ICA took part in the rising along with the Irish Volunteers. Across the road from Liberty Hall, is a fine statue of James Connolly, behind which is the plough and the stars, once depicted on the militia's banner.

Walk west towards O'Connell St. At the O'Connell Monument, look closely at one of the seated bronze winged Victories on the north-east corner. She has an indelicate bullet hole in her right breast, a legacy of 1916. Continue down to the General Post Office (GPO), with its imposing classical façade (1818, by Francis Johnston). This was the headquarters of the insurgents. Destroyed during the rising, it was rebuilt in 1924-29. Commemorative ceremonies are held here every Easter.

Inside is the bronze figure of Cú Chulainn, a legendary Irish warrior. The story runs that he bound himself to a tree to maintain courage in the face of death. His enemies were too scared to approach until he was dead, as proved by the raven on his shoulder.

Within is the An Post Museum. The section on the rising, in this, the centre of it all, is risibly sparse. However, the one display on this theme, a 3D video of events, is presented in an interesting way.

Figure with bullet hole in breast

Bust of Patrick Pearse at St Enda's

Taking advantage of Britain's engagement in the First World War, around 1,200 insurgents moved on Easter Monday, 1916, to seize central Dublin. Patrick Pearse read the proclamation of the Irish Republic outside the GPO, which became the rebels' headquarters.

Fighting continued for a week. Finally, after five days of heavy fighting, the rebels surrendered. Shortly afterwards, 15 of the rebels were executed. There had not been initial public support for the rising, but the resultant wave of sympathy after the executions propelled the struggle for independence to its final phase. Ireland gained independence in 1922, but a bitter Civil War (1922-23) followed.

Other essential places to see: **Kilmainham Gaol** (p.66), where most of the executions took place; **The National Museum** at Collins Barracks (p.48): exhibitions on the rising. Nearby also, is the **1916 Plaza** at Arbour Hill (p.49); **The Pearse Museum** at St Enda's, Rathfarnham (p.103); **The Garden of Remembrance**, Parnell Square East (p.101).

Dublin Pubs

Left: Doheny & Nesbitt; Right: The Long Hall

Part of the essence of Dublin is its old public houses. Many have been altered but there are a number of fine 19th-century pubs still intact. A dark interior, mahogany, mirrors and a long counter are the characteristics of a Victorian public house.

Within these dark confines, there is the probability of engaging in conversation with one of the locals. Another characteristic of Dublin is its wit and, maybe, wisdom: strong opinions on life expressed in a witty manner. Come here if you want to discover the more human face of the city. In addition, they say that Guinness served in Dublin is the best in the world. The pubs noted here take pride in their pint of stout.

Here is a small selection of public houses, which are still mostly untouched and maintain the essential character of the Dublin pub:

Doheny & Nesbitt, 4-5 Lower Baggot St, D2. ☏*01 6762945*. Victorian ambience – dark fittings, mirrors and snugs (small, more private rooms where you can have a quiet drink, used to be a male preserve). The haunt of economists and politicians, there was even a joke about the 'Doheny & Nesbitt's School of Economics'. The economic theories which led to the Celtic Tiger have proved to be rather lacking, so console yourself with a good pint here.

The Long Hall, 51 South Great George's St, D2. ☏*01 4751590*. The quintessential old Dublin Pub. Literally laid out in the form of a long rectangle, as

Left: Mulligan's; Right: Toner's

WINES & SPIRITS

the name suggests. This has it all: mahogany, mirrors and the long counter.

Mulligan's. Poolbeg St, D2. ☎ *01 6775582*. Established in the 18th century. Mentioned in *Counterparts*, a short story in Joyce's *Dubliners*. Basic interior, but a pleasant haven, up a minor street in the heart of the city. Observe the plaque on the wall for 'The Society for the Preservation of the Dublin Accent' (which used to hold meetings here).

Neary's. 1 Chatham St, D2. ☎ *01 6778596*. Late-Victorian, with two distinctive ornamental arms holding lamps, inviting you inside. Comfortable interior, with large mirror to observe the surroundings.

The Stag's Head: 1 Dame Court, D2. ☎ *087 1242399*. A late-Victorian pub, the first in Dublin to enjoy the new-fangled electric light. During the day beams of light stream in through stained glass windows, some decorated with the eponymous stag's head. The mahogany bar is capped with red Connemara marble. Full of atmosphere, it's a fine place for a pint.

Ryan's, Parkgate St, D8. ☎ *01 6776097*. Victorian to the core, this pub has clocked up over 125 years of history. A place to call in if you are visiting the Phoenix Park or the Museum at Collins Barracks.

John Kavanagh's (The Gravediggers), 1, Prospect Square, near Glasnevin Cemetery, *www.thegravediggerspub.com*. Very atmospheric – this is a perfectly preserved ancient pub with good pints and tasty food. No TV or canned music.

The Brazen Head, 20 Bridge St Lower, D8. ☎ *01 6779549*. Reputed to be Ireland's oldest pub, dating from 1198. Referred to in Joyce's Ulysses: *you got a decent enough do in the Brazen Head.* Patrons are said to have included everyone from Jonathan Swift, Wolfe Tone, Daniel O'Connell to Michael Collins.

And for something totally different, **The Library Bar**, Central Hotel, 1-5 Exchequer St, D2. ☎ *01 6797302*. Located in a spacious bright room on the first floor of the hotel. You can relax here, in what looks like a gentlemen's club, with comfortable sofas and walls lined with books. It has a modern touch: WiFi.

Amongst the many, some other pubs worth considering: Toner's; The Old Stand; McDaid's; Kehoe's; Grogan's; The International Bar.

The Gravediggers, Glasnevin

Left: The Abbey Theatre, Right: The Gate Theatre

To experience world-class drama, come to Dublin with its long theatrical tradition. Principal theatres include:

Abbey Theatre, 26 Lower Abbey St, D1. ☎ *01 8872200, www.abbeytheatre.ie, is* the Irish National Theatre. Founded by the poet W. B. Yeats and Lady Gregory, it opened in 1904 with a mission to promote innovative Irish and international theatre. There were riots in 1907 in response to the use of the word 'shifts' in J. M. Synge's *The Playboy of the Western World*. Seán O'Casey's *Plough and the Stars* was put on in 1926 and depicted prostitution in Dublin. Perceived as criticising the purity of the 1916 Rising, there was another riot in the audience. Yeats harangued them from the stage: *you have disgraced yourselves again*!

The Peacock Theatre, a smaller venue in the basement, puts on more youthful plays than its elder sibling upstairs.

Gate Theatre, Cavendish Row, Parnell Square, D1. ☎ *01 8744045, www.gate-theatre.ie.* This historic theatre, housed in a fine Georgian building, was created by the theatrical duo of Micheál MacLiammóir and Hilton Edwards in 1928. It was here that the young Orson Welles got his first professional acting role and where James Mason and Michael Gambon started their careers. Nowadays, it produces European and American theatre and also Irish classics. It has developed an expertise in presenting the plays of Samuel Beckett. In 1991, the Gate became the first theatre in the world to present a full retrospective of the 19 stage plays of Beckett, which went on to New York and London. In 2008, the Gate brought a Beckett production starring Ralph Fiennes, Barry McGovern and Liam Neeson, to the Lincoln Centre Festival in New York. The Gate has presented

Spectacular show at the Gaiety

four major festivals of Harold Pinter's work. In 2008, its production of *No Man's Land* transferred to London's West End and received three Olivier Award nominations.

Gaiety Theatre, South King St, D2. ☎ *01 6795622, www.gaietytheatre.ie.* It opened in 1871, with the Lord Lieutenant (or Viceroy) of Ireland as guest of honour, to a performance of Oliver Goldsmith's comedy *She Stoops to Conquer*. This is a perfect example of a 19th-century theatre, with plush red upholstery, gilt and ornamental plasterwork. Here you have it all: the different layers of seats rising to the highest level, known as the 'Gods'. Tiers of colonnaded boxes flank the stage. It also has some fine bars, where one can partake of refreshment during the intervals.

Olympia, 72, Dame St, D2. ☎ *01 6793323, www.olympiatheatre.ie*. This theatre shows its Victorian origins, from the cast-iron stained-glass canopy of the entrance portico, to the three tiers and plush red decor inside. It started off as the 'Star of Erin' and was later known as 'Dan Lowry's Music Hall'. As well as theatrical performances, it presents a wide range of musical shows.

Canopy at the Olympia

Bord Gáis Energy Theatre

Theatres abound in Dublin. Other worthwhile performance and theatrical venues include: **The Bord Gáis Energy Theatre**, Grand Canal Square, Docklands, D2. ☎ *01 6777999, www.grandcanaltheatre.ie* (p.97); **The O2**, North Wall Quay, D1. ☎ *01 8198888, www.theo2.ie*; **Bewley's Café Theatre**, 2nd Floor, 78 Grafton St, D2. ☎ *01 6727720, www.bewleyscafetheatre.com;* **Tivoli Theatre**, 138 Francis St, D8. ☎ *01 4544472, www.tivoli.ie;* **Samuel Beckett Theatre**, Trinity College, D2. ☎ *01 8961000, www.tcd.ie/Drama*

Temple Bar (page 43) theatres include: **Project Arts Centre**, 39 East Essex St. ☎ *01 8819613, www.projectartscentre.ie;* **New Theatre**, 43 East Essex St. *01 6703361, www.thenewtheatre.com;* **The Ark Children's Theatre**, 11a Eustace St. ☎ *01 6707788, www.theark.ie.*

Further out: **The Helix**, DCU, Collins Avenue, Glasnevin, D9. *www.thehelix.ie*; **Pavilion Theatre**, Dún Laoghaire. *www.paviliontheatre.ie*; **Civic Theatre**, Tallaght, D24. *www.civictheatre.ie;* **Mill Theatre**, Dundrum, D16. *www.dundrum.ie/theatre.*

27 Churches: 19th-Century Sublimity

Left: St Paul's; Right: St Audoen's

There are many fine churches in Dublin. This short walk includes a small selection. Note that if you enter a church, please do so respectfully.

Start off on the south bank of the Liffey, walk up to Usher's Quay, past the white James Joyce Bridge. Look north across the river: observe the classical **St Paul's** Catholic Church on Arran Quay, with its fine frontage reflected in the river. Called *an example of heroic post-Emancipation classicism*, this church, designed by Patrick Byrne, was completed in 1844 (see panel regarding Emancipation).

Retrace your steps, heading west, and turn right up Lower Bridge St. Further up the hill, on the left down Cook St, you can see the last surviving city gate, part of the 13th-century city wall.

Continue up to High St. On the left is the entrance to (old) **St Audoen's** and its visitor centre. The only surviving medieval parish church in Dublin, the original Anglo-Norman building dates from around 1200. It is dedicated to St Ouen the 7th-century patron saint of Normandy. Within is an exhibition on St Audoen's Church within the medieval city. Part of the building is still in use as a parish church. It is worth while visiting it to experience medieval Dublin and to also see a perfectly preserved Victorian church interior, still in use as a parish church. Open May-Oct: daily 9.30am-5.30pm.

Further east along High St stands the (modern) St Audoen's Church, which was completed in 1846. Like St Paul's it is another post-Emancipation church that is classical in design and in a prominent position – and was also designed by Patrick Byrne. The interior is grand, with allusions to a Roman temple. It is now used by the Polish Catholic community.

Now walk west along Thomas St. The tall spire of the Augustinian **Church of Saints Augustine and John** comes into view. Construction began in 1862. It fully demonstrates the verticality of the English architect Augustus Pugin's intense Gothic style, then in vogue. It was designed by George Ashlin and Pugin's son Edward. The Victorian art critic John Ruskin said, on viewing the plans, that it would be *a poem in stone.* Enter the church to appreciate its soaring ceiling.

Retrace your steps a little to the west and turn right, down Francis St. Observe the frontage of the Iveagh Markets on the left. Now closed, it dates from 1906. The heads on the carved keystones represent the continents.

Continue south and to the left you see **St Nicholas of Myra** Church, stepped back a little from the street. It is sited on a former 13th-century Franciscan friary (hence the name, Francis St) and dates from 1834, to a design by John Leeson. The church is a good example of the prevailing classical style. The ceiling plasterwork is a work of art. One of the panels depicts the coat of arms of the Isle of Man. With links between Manx Catholics and Dublin dating back to the Reformation, the Isle of Man was included in the diocese of Francis St until 1850.

Back to more temporal matters and you can finish by visiting the many antique shops on Francis St, and maybe spot a bargain.

St Nicholas of Myra

Church of Saints Augustine & John

The number and type of churches in Dublin have been dictated by the religious and political ferment that swirled around Ireland over the centuries.

The Penal Laws enacted in the 1690s onwards severely restricted the Catholic and Dissenter population. Catholic churches in Dublin were outlawed and priests had to operate discreetly. In contrast, many fine Anglican (Established) churches were built in the city during the 18th century.

Catholic Emancipation, enacted in 1829, abolished the last of the restrictions and released a pent-up demand. Over the subsequent decades, there was a frenetic burst of building of Catholic churches. These were in a declamatory style and in prominent locations.

These imposing churches all over Dublin, with all their commanding classical or Gothic frontages, are a testimony to the new reality of the Victorian era, the growing influence (and future power) of the Catholic majority.

Liffey Bridges Walk

Left: Ha'penny Bridge; Right: View from Grattan Bridge

The Liffey was wide and hard to cross, hence Dublin's name in Irish, *Baile Átha Cliath*, the town of the ford (*Áth*) of the hurdles. The city's expansion is told in the history of its bridges. We look at a selection, taking a pleasant walk upriver starting at O'Connell Bridge. There are many more downstream, with one more due, for the *Luas*. Remember to wrap up well, as the river bank can be the coldest place in Dublin.

The original bridge connecting O'Connell St (then Sackville St) was designed by Gandon in 1795. The present one was rebuilt by 1880, reputed then to be the world's widest city bridge. Subsequently it was renamed after the nationalst leader, Daniel O'Connell, whose large monument it faces.

Walk west on the boardwalk on the north river bank along Bachelor's Walk to the most photographed structure in Dublin – the cast-iron Ha'penny Bridge, with its elliptical arch. It was constructed in 1816, manufactured of cast iron in Coalbrookdale in England. At first there was a pedestrian toll, requiring a ha'penny (hence the name) to cross.

Continue west along the boardwalk. Avert your eyes from the banal Millennium footbridge, opened in 2000. Next is Grattan Bridge (at the intersection with Capel St), The delightful cast-iron lamp stands, decorated with seahorses, date from the reconstruction of 1875, sitting on the foundations of the previous Essex Bridge. To the south are the Sunlight Chambers on the corner of Parliament St, built for the soap manufacturers Lever Brothers in 1901. The ceramic panels denote various scenes of cleanliness and washing in a Renaissance setting.

Continue west along the south quays, and we next encounter, in sequence, three masonry bridges from the Georgian era. Graceful and mainly constructed of granite, these are very much in harmony with the riverine setting, and complement the 18th-century Four Courts. First is O'Donovan Rossa Bridge, adjacent to Wood Quay. The keystone figures at the top of the elliptical arches represent, on the east face: Plenty, Anna

Fr Mathew Bridge

Livia (the personification of the river: *Abha na Life* in Irish) and Industry; on the west: Commerce, Hibernia and Peace.

Next is the elliptical-arch Fr Mathew Bridge, adjacent to Merchant's Quay, with cast-iron balusters. Continue and passing the Four Courts on the opposite bank, next is Mellows Bridge (Liam Mellows was executed in the Irish Civil War), adjacent to Usher's Quay. This is the oldest bridge in Dublin (1768), which is why the arches are of the simpler semi-circular shape.

Next are the white futuristic lines of the James Joyce Bridge, adjacent to Usher's Quay. Here is the geometric style of the fashionable Spanish engineer, Santiago Calatrava (p.97). However, is the bridge in context with its environment along the river, adjacent to the Georgian masonry-arch bridges, and in sight of the Four Courts? The bridge is adjacent to 15 Usher's Quay, fictional scene of Joyce's best short story, *The Dead*. However, Joyce, an iconoclast, might have savoured the slightly jarring feel of this example of outstanding engineering,

Rory O'More Bridge

located in the wrong place. Continue westwards and we come next to the blue-painted cast-iron bridge, now called after Rory O'More and manufactured in 1858. It was previously called the Victoria and Albert Bridge. Passing Collins Barracks, disregard the utilitarian 1980s bridge.

We finish at the Seán Heuston Bridge, one of the finest over the river, now carrying *Luas* trams. To the left is Heuston (formerly Kingsbridge) railway station. Built in 1828, the arched bridge is a fine example of cast iron which was cast in a nearby ironworks upriver. Decoration abounds: the corners of the bridge have crowns with the emblems of England, Wales, Scotland and Ireland. Note the sloping Egyptian-style granite abutments, a style that was popular in the 19th century. Like other Liffey bridges it has been renamed. There is irony in the change of name, from the original in honour of George IV, to that of Seán Heuston, one of the rebel leaders of 1916.

Left: James Joyce Bridge; Right: Plaque at Seán Heuston Bridge

Royal Hospital & IMMA • Kilmainham Gaol • Walks in Victorian Dublin • Walk
• Kilmainham Gaol • Walks in Victorian Dublin • Walk on the South Bull Wall
• Walks in Victorian Dublin • Walk on the South Bull Wall • Dún Laoghaire Pie
Dublin • Walk on the South Bull Wall • Dún Laoghaire Piers • Ride on the DA
the South Bull Wall • Dún Laoghaire Piers • Ride on the DART • Royal Hospital
Dún Laoghaire Piers • Ride on the DART • Royal Hospital & IMMA • Kilmainha
• Ride on the DART • Royal Hospital & IMMA • Kilmainham Gaol • Walks in V

Dublin

South Dublin

th Bull Wall • Dún Laoghaire Piers • Ride on the DART • Royal Hospital & IMMA
oghaire Piers • Ride on the DART • Royal Hospital & IMMA • Kilmainham Gaol
on the DART • Royal Hospital & IMMA • Kilmainham Gaol • Walks in Victorian
Hospital & IMMA • Kilmainham Gaol • Walks in Victorian Dublin • Walk on
• Kilmainham Gaol • Walks in Victorian Dublin • Walk on the South Bull Wall •
Walks in Victorian Dublin • Walk on the South Bull Wall • Dún Laoghaire Piers
ublin • Walk on the South Bull Wall • Dún Laoghaire Piers • Ride on the DART

29 Royal Hospital & IMMA 

View of the Formal Garden

The Royal Hospital is Dublin's finest 17th-century building, one of the first military hospitals in the world, now home to a fine modern art gallery.

Splendidly situated overlooking the Liffey, it has extensive grounds of 20 hectares. In recent decades it has been sensitively restored and now houses the Irish Museum of Modern Art (IMMA) – see panel.

Les Invalides in Paris, built by Louis XIV in 1676, was the inspiration for the Royal Hospital. When it was built here in Kilmainham in 1680, this was the first royal military hospital for old soldiers in Britain or Ireland. The Chelsea Hospital was built two years later in London. The archititect was Sir William Robinson, who also designed Marsh's Library. A retirement home rather than a hospital, 300 pensioners could be accommodated here (up to its closure in 1929). The original cost of the building was met by a levy on soldiers' pay – one could say that this was an early form of pension scheme. This location had a long heritage of charity and good works – it was constructed on the remains of a medieval abbey and hospital of the Knights of St John of Jerusalem. The building was built in the form of a quadrangle. The former Master's accommodation, dining room and chapel take up the north range, and the IMMA the other sides. Pause for refreshment in the excellent café in the basement on the northwest corner.

Refreshed, you can wander through the grounds. The

Decoration over west door

Formal Garden is to the north of the building, towards the river. Originally a physic garden, i.e. where medicinal herbs were grown, it was later used by the Master of the Royal Hospital as his private garden and laid out in the French style. The recent restoration maintains the features of French formal gardens with plants, sculpture and furniture. A focal point is the Gardener's House, said to have been designed by Edward Lovett Pearse who designed the original Parliament House in College Green (now the Bank of Ireland, p.34).

At the western end of the grounds is Bully's Acre, which is one of Dublin's oldest cemeteries: paupers were buried here until 1834. There is a shaft of a 10th-century granite cross here. It is thought that this was part of the medieval abbey. Brian Ború's army is reputed to have stayed here on the night before the Battle of Clontarf.

At the western entrance is the Richmond Tower (designed by Francis Johnston), moved here in 1846 from its original position by the Liffey quays.

Chapel from the quadrangle

IMMA is Ireland's national institution for the presentation of modern and contemporary art. Here you can see a wide and stimulating variety of art. As well as the permanent collection, there are frequent exhibitions, with displays of world-class artists' work.

Come here to be engaged, delighted or confused by the art on show. The setting is superb, in the carefully (and tastefully) refurbished old building. The long corridors, large rooms and high windows, located in the former quarters of the army pensioners, present an ideal space to display the art.

Entrance gate on Military Road

IMMA, Royal Hospital, Military Rd, Kilmainham, D8.
☏01 6129900
www.imma.ie

Opening times:
Tues-Sat 10am-5.30pm (Wed from 10.30am)
Sun 12am-5.30pm

Admission: Free

Getting there: From Heuston, go west on St John's Rd. Take first left to entrance on Military Rd.

Bus: To Heuston Stn, 26, 51, 79, 90. **Luas:** Red Line to Heuston.

30 Kilmainham Gaol

East Wing

This is a journey to the dark side of our history, but a visit to Ireland's Bastille can be a rewarding and absorbing experience. It will help in understanding some of the deeper and hidden aspects of Irish political and social history.

Currently one of the largest unoccupied gaols in Europe, it was built in 1796. Since that date this is where most of Ireland's leaders in the struggle for independence were imprisoned, as well as a myriad of 'ordinary' prisoners. The gaol was always seen as a symbol of oppression and the new Free State Government decommissioned it in 1924. Nevertheless, it was not to close without some dark deeds, post-independence – the first Republican prisoners to be executed by the Government during the Irish Civil War faced the firing squad here in November, 1922.

This is an atmospheric building, constructed in appropriately gloomy grey granite. As you enter through the front gate, under a stone carving of five writhing serpents, you can get the feeling of 'abandon hope all ye who enter here'. The cells of the west wing in the older part of the gaol are tiny. Prisoners (men, women and children) were crammed in here under appalling conditions. Things improved in 1861 when the east (or Victorian) wing was added. This utilised the latest ideas of the time on 'humane' prisons. Here the high and spacious

Carving over entrance gate

galleries are in marked contrast to the west wing. You can inspect the cells, including the spacious one where Charles Stewart Parnell, the leading nationalist politician of the late 19th century, was locked up for a short while in 1881-2.

Public hangings took place outside the gaol when it first opened. In 1891 a hanging cell was installed on the first floor, between the west and east wings. The gaol has been used as a set for many TV dramas and films, including *The Italian Job*.

Access to Kilmainham Gaol is by guided tour only. This includes an audio-visual show and a visit to an exhibition which sets out the political and penal history of the prison.

Aerial view of Gaol

Inchicore Rd, Kilmainham, D8
☎01 4535984

www.heritageireland.ie/en/dublin/kilmainhamgaol

Opening times:

Apr-Sept: Daily 9.30am-6pm

Oct-Mar: Mon-Sat 9.30am-5.30pm; Sun 10am-6pm

Admission: €6

Getting there: About 3.5km west from centre of Dublin.

Bus: 79, 79A, 78A & 51B from Aston Quay.

Stonebreakers' Yard

A major insurrection took place in central Dublin in Easter 1916 (see 1916 Walk p.52). During its aftermath the Gaol here played a sobering and grisly part.

The leaders of the rising were condemned to death by a military court and 14 of the executions were carried out here. As part of the Gaol tour there is a visit to the prison chapel. Here, the rebel Joseph Plunkett married Grace Gifford on the eve of his execution. Passing the dark cells of the west wing where the leaders of the rising were held, continue on to the bleak and high-walled Stonebreakers' Yard, where the firing squad did its work.

In early May 1916, 13 of the rebels were shot here at a point now marked by a cross. Another cross marks the spot near the gate where, on 12 May, the last execution took place. The commander of the Citizen Army and labour leader, James Connolly (with a severe leg wound), was brought in by ambulance, tied to a chair and shot.

Walks in Victorian Dublin

Doorways on Elgin Road

These relaxed walks in the southern suburbs offer an opportunity to look at some fine Victorian houses.

Ballsbridge. Walk from St Stephen's Green North in an easterly direction via Merrion Row. You pass several Victorian pubs, like Toner's, O'Donoghue's and Doheny & Nesbitt's. Continue along Baggot St Lower and cross the bridge over the Grand Canal. Pass the red-brick Victorian banks, restaurants and shops of Baggot St Upper. Red brick mixed with yellow terracotta abounds in the assertive late-Victorian Baggot Street Hospital (now a clinic) to the left. Continue on to Pembroke Road. Here the houses (large, three storeys over basement) are late Georgian. Turn right down Wellington Road (named after the Dublin-born Duke of Wellington). Here you see the fine houses, with large front gardens, built towards the beginning of the Victorian era. Turn second left down Elgin Rd. Here you are moving into the heartland of Victoriana. The style of the houses retains some of the classical elements of the preceding Georgian era, but a certain mid-Victorian exuberance is now evident. The Victorian notions about medievalism are expressed on or around the doorways. On many houses you can see polychromy applied (using bricks of different colours), popular during the Victorian period. Polychromy came to Dublin as a result of the Victorian enthusiasm for Venetian architecture – which in turn, had been influenced by Byzantine art and architecture.

Rathmines. If you want more of the Victorian experience, go to Rathmines (buses 14, 15, 15A, 15B, 65, 83, 140), which was the largest Victorian suburb. Look at the Town Hall,

Detail of Elgin Road doorway

Detail on Rathmines Town Hall

with its prominent red stone clock tower of 1897, its thin vertical shape due to being squeezed onto the footprint of an earlier house.

Continue south along the rather workaday Lower Rathmines Rd to where the road branches. Note the Victorian Slattery's Pub on the right. Inside, you can experience the atmospheric interior and maybe have a refreshment. Next door is a turreted red-brick building in Scottish Baronial style of 1901 (once a branch of a Belfast bank). Bear right, continue past the Garda station on the left, and still to the right, head up for a short distance along Grosvenor Rd (also worth walking along its full length).

Red brick Victoriana is now all around you. Turn right at the roundabout, up Grosvenor Place, then take the first turn left up Kenilworth Rd, which leads you onto Kenilworth Square. Walk around and enjoy the fine villas and terraces.

Kenilworth Square

Portrait of Victoria in Dublin Castle

During the long course of Queen Victoria's reign (1837-1901), Dublin slipped from being the second city of the Empire to a mere tenth place. There wasn't much industrial development, but there was a lot of change. The rise of the railway and the steamship meant that Dublin became a transport hub, with British goods dispatched around Ireland and in turn Irish agricultural produce being exported from Dublin port. The city also expanded as Ireland's administrative and financial centre.

The suburbs grew. The largest were the southern ones of Rathmines and Pembroke, (which included Ballsbridge), initially built to cater for the upper-middle classes. As these migrated south, the central city went into a slow decline.

Other Victorian buildings worth seeing include: **Kildare Street Club** (p.25); **Museum Building**, Trinity College (p.11); the banks on **Dame St** (p.34); **University Church**, St Stephen's Green (p.39); **Churches** (p.58); **Freemasons' Hall** and **Royal College of Physicians of Ireland** (p.42).

32 A Walk on the South Bull Wall

Winter evening sun on the South Bull Wall

This walk, offering exercise and bracing sea air, along a great granite sea wall into the heart of Dublin Bay, is well known to Dubliners but not to tourists. At the time of construction it was the longest sea wall in the world, and it still is one of the longest in Europe.

Set out for your nearly two km of a walk along the wall to the lighthouse at the end. Caution: avoid windy days, as the wall is quite exposed. Take care as there is no barrier at the edge of the sea wall.

The surface is uneven, as the individually carved and dovetailed blocks of granite have sunk a little relative to one another. To the south one can see the sweep of the bay, all the way down to Dún Laoghaire harbour and Killiney, against the backdrop of the Dublin Mountains, and further along are those in Wicklow. You can make out the pointed cone of the Sugarloaf Mountain. (Prominent, but at 501m, it is lower than many in the Wicklow range, with Lugnaquilla the highest at 925m)

Around you see the busy traffic of Dublin port with huge freighters and ferries sailing in and out. Dotted along the harbour approaches are various lighthouses and buoys which mark the way for

shipping. Across the harbour is the North Bull Wall. Beyond is Bull Island which formed in the 1800s. Further to the east is the rocky and heather-clad Howth Head, with the Baily lighthouse at its end. (In Joyce's *Ulysses,* Molly Bloom delivered her famous soliloquy on Howth Head.)

The Half-Moon swimming club is around half way down. Swimmers brave the waters in all weathers, a tradition still maintained by a few hardy souls. The name comes from a gun emplacement built here in 1793 named the 'Half-Moon Battery.'

Continue along the gently-curving wall and soon the Poolbeg Lighthouse, painted in red, becomes clearer. It is a remarkable structure, having survived 200 years of gales from the Irish Sea. Finally, you reach it. Like all Irish lighthouses, it is now unmanned and fully automatic. Shelter from the wind and cast your eye around the great panorama of Dublin Bay. Now take the journey back, with more than your day's quota of fresh air.

Getting there: From the roundabout at Sean Moore Rd in Irishtown, Dublin 4, go east along South Bank Rd, then first left down White Bank Rd and then along Pigeon House Rd. Go around by the generating station (the twin chimneys) then continue east with the sea on the right and finish at the beginning of the wall. Best to use car/taxi or cycle.

Poolbeg Lighthouse

In the early 18th century a primitive sea wall, made of oak piles, was built in an effort to maintain a channel for Dublin port.

The original Poolbeg Lighthouse was built in 1768. As the timber piles did not last due to wave action, a granite causeway was gradually built towards the land. The granite was hewn from Dalkey Hill, to the south, transported by boat and carefully put in place.

Captain William Bligh (of the Mutiny on the Bounty incident) had earned a justified reputation for navigation. He was invited to survey Dublin Bay and came here in September 1800. He proposed a wall on the north side of the channel, parallel with the south wall, to speed the flow of water thus increasing the natural scour, to deepen the shipping channel. It was adopted and the North Bull Wall was completed in 1830. This worked, the channel was cleared and the resultant silt flowed to form the Bull Island, to the north.

33 Dún Laoghaire Piers

West and East Piers

This is a chance to sample the interesting Victorian seaside town of Dún Laoghaire, which expanded after being connected by the world's first suburban railway in 1834. It then became the mail boat link with Britain and still is a ferryport.

Appropriately, arrive via the DART. As you exit the railway station, examine the adjacent town hall of 1878, designed in Venetian style. Eastwards, at the corner, you see the classical facade of the old station building (1844), now a restaurant. It was designed by John Skipton Mulvany (designer of Broadstone Station, p.99). He also designed some of the (rather posh) yacht clubs along here. Next are two Royal monuments: the green Victoria Fountain and further along Queen's Rd the monument to King George IV, an obelisk on four spheres. It was erected after the King's departure from here in 1821.

Walk out onto the east pier. You pass the bandstand, with fine late-Victorian ironwork. Continue along the pier, built in the early 19th century. The granite used here was hewn from the nearby quarries of Dalkey Hill.

Worthy of note are the cup anemometer (an Irish invention) and a plaque to Samuel Beckett. See also the memorial to Captain Boyd, captain of *HMS Ajax* who lost his life when heroically trying to save the crew of a brig during a storm in 1861. At the end of the pier is the battery. Originally defensive, the guns were used to give ceremonial salutes to Queen Victoria during her visits, the last being in 1900.

For more, retrace your steps and go west along Harbour Rd. You pass the futuristic glass building, HQ of the Irish Lights (who manage Irish lighthouses). Continue out along the west pier. Again all in solid granite, nearly 1.5km in length, it completes this fine sheltered harbour.

Bandstand

DART train emerges from Dalkey Tunnel

The DART (Dublin Area Rapid Transit) suburban railway is one of the treasures of Dublin. It runs all the way around Dublin Bay, south from Howth, through central Dublin, to Bray and on to Greystones.

The stretch south from Dalkey is particularly scenic and worth while. Join a southbound train and prepare for a visual treat: the train goes through the brief darkness of Dalkey tunnel and then it emerges to reveal one of the best railway vistas in Ireland. Here you can take in the full sweep of Killiney Bay – known as Ireland's Bay of Naples. If you see this on a fine day, with blue skies and sea, you will grasp the reason why. Above you on the hills of Killiney are the fine villas of the affluent. The Italian theme is continued in the nearby road names: Sorrento, Nerano and Vico.

Now it is all the way on to Bray, mainly along the coast. You can return from here or take the superb walk south to Greystones on a track (7 km, 2½ hrs, sometimes muddy, suitable shoes required) along Bray Head. On the way you pass the slightly faded Victorian hotels and seaside attractions on the seafront. Soon the heather and rocky outcrops are above you, the sea is far below, with the railway snaking around the cliffs.

Greystones, (like Bray) a 19th-century seaside town, has a golden sandy beach which stretches away to the south. After you have had enough sea air, it is worth calling into the Hungry Monk Restaurant (near the railway station) for refreshment. The DART from Greystones to Bray offers another dramatic journey along the cliffs. The train first runs through a long tunnel. As you leave the darkness, quickly look down at the ramparts with the waves down below, with seabirds whirling around. After three more tunnels the railway line descends towards Bray and onwards to Dublin.

Killiney Bay

Casino at Marino • Botanic Gardens • Glasnevin Cemetery • Northside Georgia
at Marino • Botanic Gardens • Glasnevin Cemetery • Northside Georgian Wa
Marino • Botanic Gardens • Glasnevin Cemetery • Northside Georgian Walk •
• Botanic Gardens • Glasnevin Cemetery • Northside Georgian Walk • Phoenix P
Gardens • Glasnevin Cemetery • Northside Georgian Walk • Phoenix Park • Dub
• Glasnevin Cemetery • Northside Georgian Walk • Phoenix Park • Dublin Zo
Glasnevin Cemetery • Northside Georgian Walk • Phoenix Park • Dublin Zoo •

Dublin

North Dublin

Phoenix Park • Dublin Zoo • Farmleigh • St Anne's Park • Croke Park • Casino
nix Park • Dublin Zoo • Farmleigh • St Anne's Park • Croke Park • Casino at
ark • Dublin Zoo • Farmleigh • St Anne's Park • Croke Park • Casino at Marino
blin Zoo • Farmleigh • St Anne's Park • Croke Park • Casino at Marino • Botanic
Farmleigh • St Anne's Park • Croke Park • Casino at Marino • Botanic Gardens
nleigh • St Anne's Park • Croke Park • Casino at Marino • Botanic Gardens •
• St Anne's Park • Croke Park • Casino at Marino • Botanic Gardens

35 Casino at Marino

If you have time to see only one place in Dublin, visit the Casino, one of the most exquisite small buildings of Europe, where artful subterfuge achieves perfection.

It is not a gambling casino, but named for a small house, as in the diminutive of the Italian *casa*. From the outside it looks like a simple single-roomed structure. However, inside there are three floors with 16 rooms. It was built as a place of enjoyment and relaxation for James Caulfield, the first Earl of Charlemont, on his estate. (The main estate house has long since been demolished).

The Casino was constructed, from the late 1750s to 1775, to a design by Sir William Chambers, whom the young Charlemont had befriended while on the Grand Tour in Europe (see panel). Chambers never visited Ireland, yet despite this, the completed building is a poem to perfect classicism. It is a Greek cross in plan, raised on a height with the figure of a lion guarding each corner. The precepts of proportion and form are faithfully adhered to. You can play the architectural detective spotting the clever stratagems used in the design. The windows, with convex panes, appear dark from the outside. This achieves the illusion of a single large window and one

Convex panes – dark from outside

cannot see the partitions of several rooms within. Classical proportion is also maintained by the large oak door at the entrance, with only two of the door panels actually opening. Four of the columns are hollow to allow drainage. The funerary urns on the roof are chimneys.

An excellent informative tour starts in the basement, which houses the kitchens. From here you climb the stairs to the main floor, where the grandeur of the house can be appreciated. The hardwood parquet floor in the entrance hall is exquisite, made from tropical trees which are now near extinction. The hall leads to other rooms with superb plasterwork decoration. When you ascend to the top storey you see the state room where Lord Charlemont would formally receive his guests in singular splendour.

State Room

Cherrymount Crescent , D3
☎ *01 8331618*
www.www.heritageireland.ie/en/dublin/casinomarino
Opening times:
May-Oct: daily 10am-5pm
Last admission 45 mins before closing
Admission: €3
Getting there: Off the Malahide Road, Marino, D3.
Bus: 14, 27, 27A, 42, 43

James Caulfield, the first Earl

Almost a rite of passage, the Grand Tour was engaged in by the sons of the aristocracy during the 18th century. In search of entertainment, knowledge and most probably pleasure, these young lords would set out for the European continent and tour Italy, with a few venturing as far as Greece. They would examine the old buildings, statues and other remains of ancient glory.

So it was that the young James Caulfield set out on his tour. He spent nine years visiting Italy, Greece, Turkey and Egypt. He arrived back in Ireland imbued with an enthusiasm for classicism, as well as his souvenirs of Roman statuary. While in Rome he became friendly with the architect William Chambers, who also designed the exceptional Somerset House in London. Chambers' contribution to neoclassical Dublin also includes Charlemont's townhouse on Parnell Square North (p.40).

Botanic Gardens, Glasnevin

Curvilinear Range Glasshouse

One of the delights of Dublin, the Botanic Gardens are a result of the centuries-old quest for science and knowledge. You can see exotic plants, set against and within some of the finest 19th-century glass structures to be seen in Europe.

In 1795, the Dublin Society purchased 11 hectares of land here, on the south bank of the river Tolka, to create a public botanic garden. The grounds, now the National Botanic Gardens, at present extend to 19 hectares. Dublin exploited its close links with Britain to acquire flora from far-flung places in the British Empire and elsewhere. Examples include plants from the Himalayas and pampas grass from Argentina, all acquired in the mid-19th century. Over time the gardens have earned an international reputation in the development of world horticulture. The present plant population amounts to around 20,000 species. There is a rockery and arboretum. Visit the yew collection, the Chinese shrubbery, the herb garden and the native plant collections. Wander around the grounds and enjoy the huge collection of trees, native and exotic.

Then there are the glasshouses. The jewel in the crown is the low, long Curvilinear Range. Most of this was constructed by the great Dublin ironmaster, Richard Turner, around the middle of the 19th century (see panel). Look at the graceful angle of the curved glass roof; observe the wonderful cast iron details

at the ends: lions' heads and decoration. Wander inside: the central portion shows how conifers evolved. The west wing has exotic rhododendrons from southeast Asia. The east wing contains plants from Australia, South Africa and South America. Cacti are located in the smaller glasshouse to the east.

To the south is the Palm House range (1884) by Boyd of Glasgow. Inside the temperature is tropical and the atmosphere humid. Home of great palms and orchids, you can imagine that you are somewhere in the rain forest. Also with a fine café, the Botanic Gardens are a great place to pass a lazy afternoon.

Palm House

Glasnevin, D9
☎ *01 8040300*
www.botanicgardens.ie

Opening times:
Mar-Oct: Mon-Fri 9am-5pm (Sat-Sun 10am-6pm)
Nov-Feb: Daily 9am-4.30pm

Admission: Free

Getting there: 3.5km north from centre of Dublin, off Botanic Rd.

Bus: 9, 19A, 14 from O'Connell St

Gable, Curvilinear Range

Richard Turner was a 19th-century pioneer of large iron structures. He developed skill in the wrought-iron I-beams which supported the glass panes. Turner combined the materials of the Industrial Revolution, now readily available at reasonable cost, (wrought and cast iron, as well as glass in great quantities) to form these sublime structures.

From his aptly named Hammersmith Ironworks at Ballsbridge in Dublin, he produced wonderful structures like the Palm House in the Botanic Gardens in Belfast (1839). With the architect Decimus Burton, he created his great masterpiece, the curvilinear Palm House at Kew Gardens in London in 1844-48. The 19th-century railway boom was an opportunity for Turner. Using his expertise in large-span roofs, he constructed those at Westland Row and Broadstone stations. He also provided roofs for railway stations in Britain, including Lime Street in Liverpool. His great Curvilinear Range Glasshouse (1845-69), was sensitively restored by the Office of Public Works in 1995.

37 Glasnevin Cemetery

O'Connell Monument

Glasnevin is Dublin's equivalent of Père Lachaise (the famous Parisian cemetery), full of 19th-century monuments to death. Styling itself as Ireland's necropolis, it offers a fascinating slice of Irish history and a reminder of our mortality.

It was set up in 1831, under the direction of the nationalist leader, Daniel O'Connell. The cemetery was established to be non-sectarian. However, when Mount Jerome cemetery opened in 1836 (see panel), most Protestants tended to be buried there, with Catholics being buried in Glasnevin.

Entering through the monumental Victorian gates, turn right and enter the Museum, which is an excellent introduction to the cemetery (guided tours are also available). This sparkling new building has a shop, a café and is reputedly the world's only museum within a cemetery. Start off, appropriately, underground and head for the basement. This is designated as the *City of the Dead* gallery – the exhibits show the burial practices and religious beliefs, as well as the meticulous record-keeping, of the 1.5 million people buried in Glasnevin. There is a display of the things you may (or may not) have wanted to know about, such as old techniques of grave digging. There is information on grave-robbers who plagued the cemetery in its early years. Now head up to the first floor. The *Milestone Gallery* houses special exhibitions on important historical figures. *The Timeline*, a 10-metre-long interactive panel, has details of prominent people buried in the cemetery. One can look through the panoramic window to see the location of their various graves. In the shop downstairs you can get maps for walks to see graves, themed along the lines of rebels, artists, etc. Then go into the burial grounds and wander.

The O'Connell Monument, marking the tomb of Daniel

Museum

O'Connell, dominates the cemetery. This round tower, at 57m, is the highest in Ireland and was built in 1861. Walk down the steps at the base of the monument and you can look through the bars into the crypt, decorated with mosaics of shamrocks and Celtic themes. Retrace your steps and all around, in the vicinity of the monument, there is an array of 19th-century statuary. The Victorians took death seriously: the more important you were, the grander your memorial. Here are mausolea, angels and Celtic crosses.

Another place of interest is the Republican plots. Even in death, there are many distinctions; politics still reigns here in Glasnevin.

Notable also is the elaborate Hiberno-Romanesque canopied monument, of 1888, to Cardinal McCabe, located to the left of the entrance gate.

Finglas Rd, Glasnevin, D11
☎01 8826550
www.glasnevinmuseum.ie
Museum opening times:
Mon-Fri. 10am-5pm
Sun 11am-5pm
Admission: €6
Getting there: Accessed via the Finglas Rd.
Bus: 140, 40A, 40D

To see a smaller, but equally interesting Victorian cemetery, go to **Mount Jerome** in Dublin's southern suburbs, to see the elaborate monuments, testimony to the self-aggrandisement of the Victorian middle classes.

Buried here, amongst others, are Sheridan le Fanu (see p.104), Oscar Wilde's father, as well as Bram Stoker's. Here are Greco-Roman temples, angels, urns and much more. One curiosity is the Gresham tomb where the lady was afraid of being buried alive. Consequently there is a chain from the coffin to a bell at the top of the tomb. Another tomb (the Harvie memorial) has a grieving dog atop, the dog lamenting his master who was drowning. Later when the dog died, it was buried here with its master. You can call at the office for guidance on where the graves are located.

158 Harold's Cross Rd, D6w
☎01 4971269
www.mountjerome.ie
Opening times:
Mon-Fri 8.30am-4pm
Sun 10am-4pm
Getting There: Off Harold's Cross Rd by the triangular park.
Bus: 54A, 16, 16A, 49, 49A

38 Northside Georgian Walk

Left: Georgian doorways; Right: Mountjoy Square

This walk, through once-elegant streets and buildings, allows you to see where the Georgian city began north of the Liffey early in the 18th century. Good profit was made in property and the northern parts of the city grew rapidly with fine houses and squares. It was only later in the century that development moved southwards.

Few tourists venture this way (as opposed to the southern Georgian squares) but there is a wealth of fine buildings to be seen here, albeit many in an uncared-for state. Is there a moral in this tale of earlier property decline in Ireland, not dissimilar to the recent crash, when the property bubble burst?

To start, at the north end of O'Connell St turn east up Parnell St. Take the first left. This, North Great George's St, was mainly developed from the 1770s onwards. The houses are grand: brick four-storey over basement, with granite steps leading up to elegant doors. Most of the houses have cast-iron covers for coal holes in the footpath outside. Several of the houses have been restored.

For a glimpse inside one of these houses with their characteristic plasterwork ceilings, visit No 35, the James Joyce Centre, (p.30). The north end of the street is framed by the elegant Belvedere House, in brick and stone. Originally constructed in 1786 for the Earl of Belvedere, it was the second Jesuit school which Joyce attended. Turn right and at the intersection with Temple St, look left and you see the striking St

Henrietta St

George's Church (1802), along the street (by Francis Johnston, who also designed the GPO and completed the King's Inns – see below). Continue along the run-down Gardiner Place to Mountjoy Square. This was once a fashionable part of Dublin: building started here around 1790. On all four sides are the terraced Georgian houses. Many are in poor condition and several are now mere façades. Rest here as there's a long walk ahead.

Walk north along Gardiner St Upper. Turn left at Lower Dorset St. Walk southwest around 600m along this rather desolate street until you come to the intersection of Granby Row (with the Maldron Hotel at the corner). Look north up St Mary's Place. The dark stone church here is, not surprisingly, referred to as the Black Church, dating from 1830. Local legend has it that if you recite the 'Hail Mary' and walk backwards around the church at midnight you will meet the Devil. Not recommended!

Continue on 250m along Upper Dorset St to Bolton St. Just before the large pile that is the Dublin Institute of Technology, turn right up the broad Henrietta St. In its heyday, the street contained some of the grandest houses on the north side of the city. How the mighty have fallen – some of these impressive houses are in poor repair. Many houses became slum tenements in the past: landlords ripped out the fine fittings and sold them off. Not all is lost; a few brave souls have restored their houses.

The street terminates in a granite triumphal archway. This marks the King's Inns, location of the professional body for barristers (lawyers entitled to appear in court) and where they eat their compulsory meals. Walk under the arch to the spacious grounds at the front. It dates from 1800, to a design by James Gandon (p.50), completed in 1817 by Francis Johnston.

Finally, it is worth having a look westwards at the former Broadstone railway station (p.99). On a height and in poor surroundings, this is set back from Constitution Hill and is the finest but most neglected Victorian building in Dublin.

King's Inns

39 Phoenix Park

Herd of Deer

Located around three km to the west of the city centre, the Phoenix Park was created as a royal deer-park from 1662 onwards. At 707 hectares it is one of the largest enclosed recreational spaces in any European capital city. Over the years, a diverse mix of buildings and institutions have been built all over the park, making for an interesting walk of discovery. Join the Dubliners who stroll or jog here and enjoy the fresh air in the wide open spaces.

Enter from Parkgate St and continue up the great diagonal Chesterfield Avenue, which bisects the park. As one enters, immediately to the right is the People's Garden. These nine hectares date from 1864 and include ornamental lakes, a children's playground, a picnic area and flowerbeds. Visit here to see Victorian horticulture at its best. Behind the garden is Dublin Zoo (p.86). On the eastern boundary is the headquarters of the Irish police, the Garda Síochána, a fine, if rather forbidding 19th-century building. Understandably, you cannot enter here! The McKee army barracks further north along this boundary is also out of bounds. A delightful confection of red-brick turrets with a touch of the Raj, dating from 1888, you can just get a sight of it from afar.

Retrace your steps to the main avenue: to the south is the towering granite obelisk of the Wellington Testimonial. Over the first half of the 19th century, loyal citizens subscribed for this monument to Dublin-born Arthur Wellesley, first Duke of Wellington. Above the stepped base, the plaques around the pedestal depict the Duke's victories and are cast from cannon captured during the Napoleonic wars.

Wellington Testimonial

Continue along Chesterfield Avenue, passing the cricket grounds to the left and the polo ground to the right. Halfway along the avenue, in the middle of a roundabout, is the Phoenix Column (of 1747), a fluted Corinthian column capped with a ferocious phoenix. Phoenix, the name adopted for the park, has a fine ring to it, but it is a rather clumsy anglicisation of the name of the well said to have been located here, *fionn uisce* or clear water. Off to the right is the former vice-regal lodge, now the residence, *Áras an Uachtaráin*, of the President of Ireland, currently Michael D. Higgins.

To the southwest is the residence of the American ambassador. This fine mansion was the former Chief Secretary's Lodge, built in 1776.

Northwest off this roundabout is Ashtown Castle with a visitor centre which tells the story of the park through the ages. It is worth getting a map of the park here. (On Saturdays you can apply here for tours of *Áras an Uachtaráin*, if available.) Behind the visitor centre you can find the large Victorian walled garden.

Back along the avenue, among the trees you can usually see the resident herd of fallow deer. To the left the Papal cross can be seen, marking where Pope John Paul II said mass for a million people in 1979.

Continue along the avenue

Phoenix Column

to the next crossroads. If you turn left here down Ordnance Survey Rd, not surprisingly, you will see the Ordnance Survey on the right. This institution mapped Ireland from the early 19th century. The rather severe architecture shows its military origins. It is possible to buy maps of Ireland in the sales shop here, of all scales and sections.

With a map of the park, you can now wander among its other nooks and crannies – a true cornucopia of hidden delights. There are many historic buildings in the grounds including gate lodges and a magazine fort, not to mention the trees, ponds, and glens. You can visit Farmleigh (along White's Rd, off Ordnance Survey Rd, p.88).

8 Parkgate St, D8
☎ *01 6770095*

www.phoenixpark.ie

Opening times:

Main gates at Parkgate St and Castleknock are open 24 hours. Other gates 7am-11pm.

Bus: 46A to North Circular Rd Gate. 25, 26 to Parkgate St. **Luas:** Heuston or Museum stop.

40 Dublin Zoo

Located within Phoenix Park, Dublin Zoo was founded in 1830. This is the world's third oldest public zoo, as it opened just after those in Paris and London. This new institution fitted squarely with the contemporary hunger for science, knowledge and improvement. It also helped that the British Empire was expanding, with access to yet more strange lands and exotic creatures. The zoo today has many fine refurbished Victorian buildings. Noteworthy are the original thatched entrance lodge, the Roberts House and the timber loggia of the Haughton Memorial building (see panel).

There has always been an affinity between Dubliners and what they call the 'Ah-zoo'. In 1831 there were only five species on display: two ostriches from Africa, one samber deer from India, two wapiti deer, two emus from Australia and two passenger pigeons from America. From these small beginnings of less than two hectares, it has expanded greatly to 28 hectares, benefitting from the large amount of space available within the park. This now affords an opportunity to see a huge range of wild animals.

Using the latest concepts in zoo management, many animals can be observed in naturalistic spaces with vegetation and water features reflecting their native habitats. Being in natural social groups, the animals are able to breed and raise their own young. For example, animals of African origin are free to roam in the African Plains area, which

covers 13 hectares.

From 1855 when it acquired its first lion, Dublin Zoo gained an international reputation for expertise in breeding lions. There is a story that a Dublin lion was one of those that can be seen roaring at the start of the old MGM films.

There are exhibitions which give explanation and context to various aspects of animals and nature. It is not all heavy stuff, however: it is a great and enjoyable place to wander around in any weather.

Phoenix Park, D8
☎01 4748900
www.dublinzoo.ie
Opening times:
Daily. Mar-Sept 9.30am-6pm
Feb 9.30am-5pm; Oct 9.30am-5.30pm; Nov-Jan 9.30-4pm
Admission: €15.50
Getting there: access from the Phoenix Park.
Bus: 25, 25A, 26, 46A, 66, 66A, 66B, 67, 67A, 68, 69
LUAS: Red Line, 15 minutes from the Museum or Heuston stops.

Haughton Memorial Building

One of the early guiding lights was **Samuel Haughton**, who was president of the Zoological Society in the 1860s, and is commemorated by the building named after him.

A clergyman, he was an extraordinary polymath, having three doctorates. He was Professor of Geography at Trinity College and President of the Royal Irish Academy.

He took a medical degree at the age of 40. He calculated the age of the earth as 2,300 million years. That was pretty close for his era, as current estimates are at around 4,500 million years.

However, it was in the macabre area of hanging that he pushed the boundaries of practical science. Previously an excessive length of rope could decapitate a condemned person; too short and the person would strangle. Haughton established a more humane method, developing a mathematical table which became known as 'Haughton's Drop', which became standard practice in the 1870s. It allowed calculation of the correct drop to ensure a swift death.

Farmleigh

Though not part of the Phoenix Park (p.84), Farmleigh is tucked away discreetly at its north-west boundary and accessed from the park.

In 1873, the grounds were acquired by Edward Cecil Guinness on his marriage to his cousin, Adelaide Guinness. He was a great-grandson of Arthur Guinness, the founder of the brewery. Edward Cecil became the first Earl of Iveagh in 1919. The original house was small, dating from the 18th century and was rebuilt by the Guinnesses.

Inside the house (access by guided tour only) are many fine rooms like the ballroom and large conservatory. The galleried library is particularly impressive. The interior decoration could be generally described as 'rich man's eclecticism'.

The property was bought by the State in 1999 and renovated with the intention of providing a place for State visitors. It is possible for the public to visit most of the time, however.

The grounds offer an opportunity for a pleasant ramble. Nineteenth-century buildings include the luxurious dairy complete with stained glass. There is a small lake, with a boathouse, now a café. The gardens include a glasshouse and decorative flowerbeds.

A striking feature is the tall Italianate tower to the west (1880), which dominates the surrounding countryside. Water from the nearby river Liffey was pumped into storage tanks within the tower, which has a large clock on each side. There was a local rhyme:

Mister Guinness had a clock
And on its top a weather cock
To show the people
Castleknock.

Library

Castleknock, D5
☏ *01 8155900*

www.farmleigh.ie

Opening times:

Daily 10am-5pm

Tours of house: Thurs-Sun

Admission: Free

Getting there: From Parkgate go along Chesterfield Ave, at the third roundabout turn left and then first right.

Bus: 37 to Castleknock Gate. Enter the Phoenix Park and take the pedestrian pathway to your immediate right. Follow the signs. Farmleigh is a 15-minute walk.

The Phoenix Park gets all the attention, but St Anne's Park is another wonderful wide-open expanse on the north side of Dublin with parklands and lots of interesting features.

This is another of the great Guinness estates. From 1835 onwards the family built up a large estate in the Raheny area. It was eventually sold to Dublin Corporation in the 20th century. Within its 110 hectares are green expanses, sports fields, tennis courts and a golf course, with a central grand avenue. There is a profusion of flowers and trees. Notable is the award-winning Rose Garden. Dublin's city arboretum is here, with 1,000 species of trees.

Dotted throughout are charming reminders of the gilded life of the Guinnesses. The Red Stables are a fine example of late 19th-century Tudor style, with a courtyard and surrounding stables. It is now refurbished and in use as artists' studios. Also within is an excellent café with a glass roof.

Red Stables

Wander northeast to the Clock Tower Garden. Inside is the Miniature Rose Garden. On a westwards stroll into the woods, you come across the small Naniken river which flows through the park to the ornamental pond. Continue along until you reach the pond with a derelict boathouse in vaguely classical style. Climb a pathway up a rise on which is located the three-storey Roman Tower, recently restored from its layer of graffiti. It was designed by Sir Benjamin Lee Guinness and is a copy of the Tomb of the Julii (from Roman Gaul).

Roman Tower

Raheny, D5
☎ *01 8331859*

Opening Times:
Winter: 10am-5 pm
Summer: Closing time varies

Getting there: entrances at All Saints Rd; Watermill Rd; Mount Prospect Rd and James Larkin Rd (on the coastal road to Howth).

Bus: 130, 29A

43 Croke Park

Croke Park Stadium

'An iconic symbol of Ireland' is one of the descriptions used during the visit in 2011 of Queen Elizabeth II to Croke Park. Visit this giant stadium to get a deeper insight into what is a great passion of many Irish people.

This is the home of the Gaelic Athletic Association (GAA) which organises the playing of Gaelic games. These are indigenous to Ireland (also played in such outliers as the USA and Australia!) and are the most popular games across the island. Hurling is one such, a game with a curved stick (a *camán*) and a small leather ball (a *sliotar*), reputed to be one of the fastest field games in the world. Gaelic football is much more energetic than soccer (dare one say, more exciting?) and the ball can be handled. This 80,000 capacity stadium is where major matches are held. In September every year, Dublin hums with excitement and bustle, when the All-Ireland Finals are held here for both Hurling and Gaelic Football.

One of the reasons for the fuss during the Queen's visit is historical: in 1920 during Ireland's War of Independence, British troops fired on part of the crowd attending a match here. They killed 14 people (in retaliation for assassinations earlier that day), an event known as Bloody Sunday.

The stadium (the third largest in Europe) dominates the small terraced houses of the neighbourhood. Beneath the Cusack stand is the GAA Museum which was established

Gaelic Football

to commemorate the contribution to Irish sporting, cultural and social life made by the GAA since its foundation in 1884. The museum is open daily throughout the year. It deals with the growth of the GAA at home and abroad and its unique role in the cultural revival and national movement in Ireland. It contains a large display of hurleys, jerseys, trophies and banners that illustrate the development of Gaelic games from ancient times to the present. There is an interactive games area and a café.

For a behind-the-scenes look at this grand arena you can take a guided tour which takes about 1hr 20min.

Exhibition

Jones's Rd, D3

☎ *01 8192300*

www.crokepark.ie

Opening times: Check website

Tour (incl museum): €12

Getting there: Croke Park is located in north Dublin between Drumcondra and Ballybough. Access to the GAA Museum is via St Joseph's Avenue, just off Clonliffe Rd.

Bus: 3, 11, 11A, 16, 16A from O'Connell St to Drumcondra Station (10 minutes' walk).

Aviva Stadium

Other sports include:

Rugby (and international soccer) at the recently-built Aviva Stadium in Lansdowne Road. Futuristic and state-of-the-art, it has a seated capacity of 50,000. *www.avivastadium.ie*, tour of the stadium, €10.

All Ireland Polo Club, Phoenix Park, founded in 1873, the second oldest in Europe.

The Phoenix **Cricket** Club (founded 1830) in Phoenix Park. Cricket is also played in Trinity College, Clontarf and Rathmines.

Golf courses include: Portmarnock Links, Portmarnock, Co. Dublin. *www.portmarnock.com;* Royal Dublin, Dollymount, Co. Dublin. *www.theroyaldublingolfclub.com;* Elm Park Golf Club, Nutley Lane, D4. *www.elmparkgolfclub.ie.*

Horses: racing at Leopardstown Racecourse, D19. *www.leopardstown.com.*

Show Jumping: Royal Dublin Society Horse Show, early August. *www.dublinhorseshow.com*

Portmarnock Links

Hire a Bike • Kids' Dublin • Docklands Ramble • Five Dublin Railway Termini •
Docklands Ramble • Five Dublin Railway Termini • Dublin & War • Miscellany
Dublin Railway Termini • Dublin & War • Miscellany of Museums • Ghoulish
Dublin & War • Miscellany of Museums • Ghoulish Dublin • Hire a Bike • Kid
of Museums • Ghoulish Dublin • Hire a Bike • Kids' Dublin • Docklands Rar
Dublin • Hire a Bike • Kids' Dublin • Docklands Ramble • Five Dublin Railway
Dublin • Docklands Ramble • Five Dublin Railway Termini • Dublin & War • M

Dublin

Around Dublin

Var • Miscellany of Museums • Ghoulish Dublin • Hire a Bike • Kids' Dublin •
s • Ghoulish Dublin • Hire a Bike • Kids' Dublin • Docklands Ramble • Five
re a Bike • Kids' Dublin • Docklands Ramble • Five Dublin Railway Termini •
Docklands Ramble • Five Dublin Railway Termini • Dublin & War • Miscellany
Dublin Railway Termini • Dublin & War • Miscellany of Museums • Ghoulish
ublin & War • Miscellany of Museums • Ghoulish Dublin • Hire a Bike • Kids'
Museums • Ghoulish Dublin • Hire a Bike • Kids' Dublin • Docklands Ramble

44 Hire a Bike

Using the *Dublinbikes* scheme can be one of the best-value experiences on offer in the city. It's not expensive and Dublin is flat and easy to cycle around. The scheme is organised for the city by JCDecaux, which manages a similar scheme in Paris.

The bikes are natty pieces of equipment (albeit a bit heavy), with a basket, bell, lights and lock. The three-day ticket, (costs €2, free hire for the first 30 minutes, after that, charges per hour of use) is best, using your credit card at one of the 15 stations with credit card terminals. There are 44 stations in all, mainly distributed around the inner city. When you have finished, leave the bike at any station – for locations see *www.dublinbikes.ie* (or the App *dublinbikes*). ☎ *1850 777070.*

If parking elsewhere in the meantime, always lock the bike. Dublin, regrettably, is bike-theft central. Be careful: there are many cycle lanes in Dublin, but all – cyclists, pedestrians and motorists – are bad on road safety. You have to allow for the rhythm of indiscipline on the roads and cycle paths. Ideally wear a helmet and have waterproof clothing handy.

Some of Dublin's attractions can be easily seen by bike: Gandon on the Liffey (p.50); Railway Termini (p.98); the Liffey Bridges (p.60), Northside Georgian (p.82).

For a full day: cycle to Kilmainham Gaol (p.66) then the Royal Hospital Kilmainham (p.64), followed by the Guinness Storehouse (p.44)

For trips by the sea: *Northside* – cycle to Clontarf Rd and on to Howth. En route, visit Bull Island and its long beach. Also call into St Anne's Park (p.89); *Southside* – cycle to Ringsend, then through Irishtown along Sean Moore Rd to the roundabout and on to the South Bull Wall (p.70).

Left: Aquatic Centre; Right: Wax Museum

Attractions for children abound. Here is an assortment:

National Wax Museum Plus. Most eclectic exhibition in Dublin. Crammed into four floors are wax characters from history and entertainment plus a Children's Fantasy World. The Armoury, Foster Place, D2. *www.waxmuseumplus.ie.*

National Aquatic Centre. Located in Blanchardstown to the northwest of the city (bus 38, 38A). This is one of Europe's biggest indoor water parks. Attractions include the Wave Pool and the Lazy River. *www.nationalaquaticcentre.ie.*

Natural History Museum The Victorian ambience is hard to beat – one of the most entertaining places for children, with free admission (p.20).

The Ark in Temple Bar is Europe's first custom-designed arts centre for children (p.56). *www.ark.ie.*

Viking Splash Tour: you don a Viking helmet and pile into a converted amphibious vehicle. En route you are encouraged to let out a few Viking war whoops. You reach the Grand Canal Dock, whereupon the vehicle becomes a boat and sails around the dock. Depart St Stephen's Green North. *www.vikingsplash.ie.*

Sea Safari: Take a high-speed tour around Dublin Bay, departing from Poolbeg Marina. The Dublin Bay North Tour takes you north out of Dublin Port. The south tour takes you along the River Liffey and south to Dún Laoghaire, Dalkey Island and Killiney Bay. *www.seasafari.ie.*

The Science Gallery, Trinity College, on Pearse St, presents science in a fresh way. Great café. *www.sciencegallery.ie*

Imaginosity!, a children's museum, located to the south of the city in the Beacon South Quarter. Interactive space for children under nine years of age and their families. *www.imaginosity.ie.*

Viking Splash afloat

46 Docklands Ramble

Left: View of docks; Right: Samuel Beckett Bridge

Take a ramble in the revitalised docklands quarter, at the mouth of the Liffey, to experience the shock of the new and some of the charm of the old.

Start off by walking from O'Connell Bridge east along the south quays. See the Custom House and IFSC across the river. Pass the Seán O'Casey footbridge, of attractive modern design.

At Sir John Rogerson's Quay, just past the Samuel Beckett Bridge, turn right up Cardiff Lane. You come to the (clumsily-named) Bord Gáis Energy Theatre, designed by Daniel Liebeskind. This is a brand-new 2,100-capacity theatre. Turn left and you enter the new development of Grand Canal Dock. A word on the new buildings you pass on the rest of the walk: these were symbolic of the thrusting Celtic Tiger. However, this ground to a crashing halt: some of the stylish apartments and office blocks are empty and some may be in the care of NAMA, an agency for bankruptcy assets.

The dock here was once a thriving hub in the early 19th century, full of barges and small ships, from the time when the canal was the only way to move heavy goods inland. This was the terminus of the Grand Canal, completed in 1796, which loops south of the inner city, still navigable to much of the south and west of Ireland.

Along the north side of Hanover Quay are cafés and restaurants and it is pleasant to take a break here. Continue east down the quay and at the end you see the three locks where the canal boats can descend from the higher dock and canal level down to the Liffey waters. You can see the names of long-forgotten Lords Lieutenant, Camden, Buckingham, and Westmoreland, carved on the stone walls.

At the Grand Canal locks

Now retrace your steps to the Samuel Beckett Bridge. This opened in 2009 and is worth travelling to see. It is a particularly successful work by the Spanish engineer, Santiago Calatrava: its shape evokes a harp, symbol of Ireland. The white, soaring, Aeolian lines of the bridge fit in with the environment of modern buildings to be found all over the docklands. The bridge swings to allow vessels upriver. (Calatrava also designed the James Joyce Bridge, p.60).

Adjacent to the bridge is the new Convention Centre with its glass atrium at the front, in the 'tilted can' style. Designed by the Irish-born US-based architect, Kevin Roche. Modish architecture? Yes. Iconic? No.

Turn right and head eastwards down North Wall Quay. Next is a skeletal office building, currently half-built. This was to have been the headquarters of the late but not lamented Anglo-Irish Bank, the bank that bankrupted Ireland, making, on the way, the largest losses ever in banking history.

Continue eastwards and you see a former lightship, painted red, moored in front of the O2 arena. Previously

Detail on bridge

a railway freight depot, now much renovated, it is a venue for major acts. It hosted the Eurovision Song Contest three times. In the contest of 1994 the short interval piece was an instant sensation, which grew into the *Riverdance* show. From the footpath of the utilitarian Eastlink bridge you have a good view downriver at the busy docks of Dublin Port, with the bay beyond.

The plaza behind the O2 is now a bleak place. With nothing more to detain you, retrace your steps along North Wall Quay. Upriver is the replica of the famine ship Jeanie Johnston based on the original of1847. This is typical of the ships which brought the people fleeing from the rigours of the Irish famine to North America in the mid-19th century. On board you can see the hard conditions that these pauperised people had to endure. *www.jeaniejohnston.ie.*

Jeanie Johnston

47 The Five Dublin Railway Termini

Left: Pearse Station; Right: Harcourt St Station

Dublin is lucky to have a surprising number of impressive Victorian railway termini which are worth seeing.
Getting around: use public transport, or hire a *Dublinbike* (p.94).

Start at **Harcourt Street Station**. (Harcourt stop on the Luas Green Line). Built in 1859, the style is Roman Baroque. Note the delightful *oeil-de-boeuf* oval windows set on high. Trains ran from here to Bray and Wexford. The line closed in 1958. The recent *Luas* light rail system was built on much of the old railway formation.

Go north up Harcourt St to St Stephen's Green West, down Grafton St and turn right along Nassau Street. Continue until you turn left for Westland Row. At the end of this street is a bridge spanning the roadway into **Pearse Station** (formerly Westland Row). This was Ireland's first station, being the original terminus of the Dublin & Kingstown Railway of 1834, the world's first suburban railway. It was reconstructed in 1891, resulting in the present rather plain frontage. It is a historic spot. Many Republican prisoners alighted here to a tumultuous welcome on their return from release in Britain during the struggle for independence in the early 20th century. The writer Flann O'Brien (known also as Myles na gCopaleen) used the station on the commute to his civil service job and enjoyed liquid refreshments in the station buffet (now closed). More prosaically, Michael Caine took a train here, in the film *Educating Rita*.

Take a DART from here to **Connolly Station** (formerly Amiens Street), on the line which runs high over the city. Crossing the Liffey by train,

Connolly Station

MGWR crest

you pass the fine 18th-century Custom House to the east. Alight at Connolly and exit via the west of the station. The building is graced by three Italianate towers, but overall it is rather grey and dour. This was the terminus for the Dublin & Drogheda Railway. Its foundation stone was laid in 1844 by the Lord Lieutenant.

Take a *Luas* Red line west from here. Alight at the Four Courts stop. Go west along Chancery St and turn right on Church St for a just-under-one-km walk towards Constitution Hill. Past a jumble of 20th-century flats, turn left. As you climb the hill you can see the the station flanked by a bus depot, parked cars in front and a petrol station in the foreground. The **Broadstone Station** is one of Dublin's finest Victorian buildings, now neglected and out of public sight. This was the terminus of the grandly-named Midland Great Western Railway (MGWR). As well as being a train station, this was the terminus and harbour (where the car park now stands) for the Royal Canal. Dating from 1850, the station building was designed by John Skipton Mulvany (other works, p.72). The façade has an Egyptian theme. The writer Maurice Craig noted that the traveller who sees it for the first time *feels as.. if he were to stumble unawares upon the monstrous silences of Karnak or Luxor.*

Retrace your steps to the *Luas* Four Courts stop. Take a tram towards **Heuston Station** (formerly Kingsbridge). It opened in 1848 and was designed by Sancton Wood as the Dublin terminus of the Great Southern & Western Railway. It is still the main gateway for train services to the south and west. The cupolas on each side give an echo of the Raj. The roof over the train platforms still has much of the original Victorian ironwork. The plaster detailing on the ceiling in the booking office, on the south, is impressive.

Left: Heuston Station; Right: Broadstone Station

Dublin & War

War Memorial Gardens

Dublin, long a garrison city, has had a lengthy relationship with war and the military. Given Ireland's chequered history, the first question on remembering the casualities of war has been: who to commemorate? The problem has been solved by having memorials to every side. There are many military memorials in Dublin. Ironically, those dedicated to the Irish who fought for the British crown are generally larger and better designed than the memorials to those who fought for Irish independence.

The following is a small selection of the many war memorials in the city:

Royal Dublin Fusiliers' Arch, St Stephen's Green (northwest corner). It commemorates the fallen of the Irish regiments of the British Army in the Second Boer War of 1899-1902. As usual with these matters, attitudes differed in Ireland and this was dubbed the 'traitors' gate' by nationalists when built in 1907

War Memorial Gardens, South Circular Rd, Islandbridge, D8. (Bus 51, 68 and 69). Set in extensive landscaped grounds, it is one of the best open spaces in Dublin and worth a visit. These gardens are dedicated to the memory of the 49,400 Irishmen who fought and died on the British side during the First World War. There are terraces, pergolas and lawns. At the ends of the walkways under the pergolas are granite book-rooms with illustrated manuscripts containing the names of the fallen. The gardens were constructed during the 1930s, and to avoid

Mosaic at Garden of Remembrance

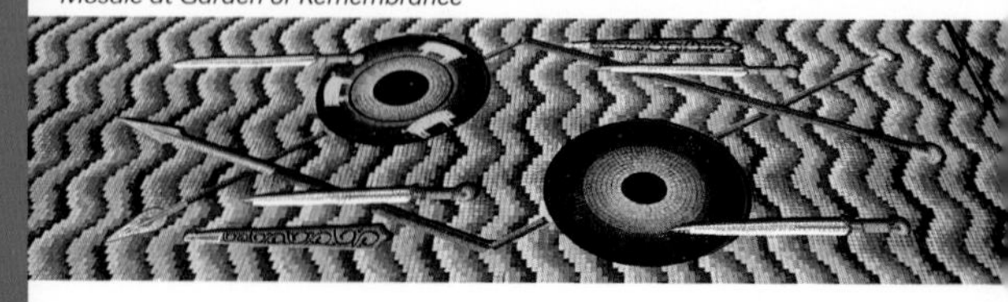

discord, the workforce was composed of half ex-British Army and half ex-Irish Army men. The designer was Sir Edward Landseer Lutyens (1869-1944). Lutyens had a good (post-) war – he received a multitude of commissions to design war memorials, including the India Arch in New Delhi.

The Garden of Remembrance, Parnell Square East. This was built in 1966 to commemorate those who gave their lives in the cause of Irish freedom. The central large sculpture is on the theme of the *Children of Lir*, from Celtic mythology. This 1960s style garden might look a bit akin to a Soviet-style war memorial, but is saved by the details: the delightful mosaics in the pool, the blooming flowers and railings decorated with harps and trumpets. Visiting heads of state come here to lay a wreath. And so it was that Queen Elizabeth II came here during her historic visit in 2011. She bravely laid a wreath here (commemorating those who fought against British rule) and laid to rest many of the awkward demons lurking around this issue.

Figures at Defence Forces Memorial

Defence Forces Memorial, Merrion Square West. Tucked away discreetly on the edge of the park, this is a charming little pyramidical structure. Through its glass windows a perpetual flame can be seen as well as figures of a sailor, airman, and soldiers, male and female, of the Irish Defence Forces. It commemorates the members of these forces who died in service. However, does it suffer from being too modest, in comparison to similar memorials in other countries?

For much more: many memorials to Irishmen who fought for the Empire in Victorian wars can be seen in **St Patrick's Cathedral** (p.16); the excellent **Soldiers and Chiefs Exhibition** in the National Museum, Collins Barracks (p.48), gives context to Ireland's diverse military history; the **1916 Memorial**, the poignant monument to the executed leaders of the Easter Rising, is at the plaza at **Arbour Hill**, behind Collins Barracks.

Left: Royal Dublin Fusiliers' Arch; Right: 1916 Memorial, Arbour Hill

Miscellany of Museums

Left: Staircase, Garda Museum: Right: Exhibit at Revenue Museum

There are lots of smaller museums in Dublin worth a visit:

Garda Museum. This sets out the history of the Irish police, the Garda Síochána, and its predecessors, the Royal Irish Constabulary and the Dublin Metropolitan Police. It contains a huge amount of interesting memorabilia, photographs and uniforms. The large amount of detail on offer results in an exhibition sometimes a little difficult to follow – the hand of a professional curator is needed. There is a wonderful spiral staircase that allows you to ascend to yet another floor to see more chapters of the police story. The building itself, the Record Tower, dating from the early 13th century, is an atmospheric nook at the back of Dublin Castle and worth experiencing. Red Hugh O'Donnell, lord of Donegal, was incarcerated here and escaped in January 1592. The tower was refurbished by Francis Johnston in 1813.

www.garda.ie
Mon-Fri 9am-5pm
Admission: Free
Dublin Castle, Lower Yard.

Revenue Museum. A well-laid-out exhibition which tells the story of revenue collecting in Ireland. It includes details of the fight against poteen-making and drug smuggling, including a disconcerting exhibit of a toilet with transparent fittings (don't ask).

www.revenue.ie
Mon-Fri 10am-4pm
Admission: Free
Chapel Crypt, Dublin Castle, Lower Yard, D2.

National Print Museum. This is a comprehensive exhibition which tells the story of how printing developed and brought information, in all its forms, to the world. Printing artefacts and many old printing presses are on display. A video tells how these were used and operated. There is a shop and the appropriately-named Gutenberg Café. It also affords an opportunity to see Beggar's

National Print Museum

Bush barracks, which dates from 1827. Once a major army barracks, it closed in the 1920s, but not before the execution here of Erskine Childers, the English author of *The Riddle of the Sands,* in 1922, during the Irish Civil War.

www.nationalprintmuseum.ie
Mon-Sat 9am-5pm; Sun 2-5pm
Admission: €3.50
Beggar's Bush Barracks on Haddington Road, D4.

Jewish Museum. Many Jews came to Dublin towards the end of the 19th century. The museum sets out the important part this small community plays in Irish life. A former synagogue, it is located in the area of Portobello, near the South Circular Rd, which once had a large Jewish population. The items on display (quite cluttered, needs to be curated properly), show the participation of the Jewish community in Ireland. Upstairs is the original synagogue with its ritual fittings and rare fabrics.

www.jewishireland.org
May-Sept: Sun-Thur 11am-3.30pm; Oct-Apr: Sun only 10.30am-2.30pm
Admission: Free, donations welcome
3 Walworth Rd, South Circular Rd, D8.

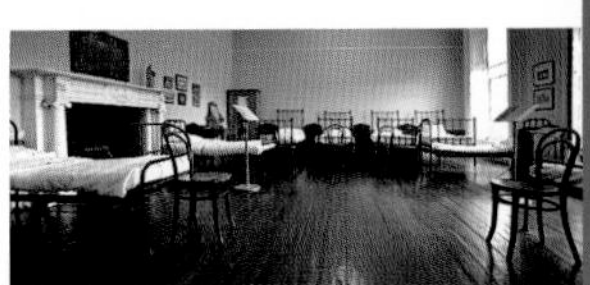

Pearse Museum. Patrick Pearse was a leader of the 1916 Rising and was executed afterwards (p.52). This fascinating character managed to combine being a revolutionary with being a poet, writer and teacher. A school was established by Pearse in this fine Georgian mansion, which was also the home of the Pearse family. It is now a well-presented museum set in extensive grounds with a riverside walk. The tour is informative and there is a good café.

☎ *01 4934208*
Mar-Oct: Mon, Wed-Sat 9.30am-5.30pm, Sun from 10am; Nov -Feb: Mon, Wed-Sat 9.30am-4pm.
Admission: Free
St Enda's Park, Grange Road, Rathfarnham, Co. Dublin.

Little Museum of Dublin. Small museum with an off-beat take on Dublin. Two rooms of 20th-century memorabilia.

www.littlemuseum.ie
Thur- Mon 12am-6pm. (Thur to 9pm)
Admission: €5
15 St Stephen's Green, D2.

Ghoulish Dublin

Left: Grave-robbers at Glasnevin; Right: Mortsafe in Drumcondra Graveyard

Experience thrills of a Gothick nature in the darker crevices of Dublin's history.

At **Glasnevin Cemetery,** see the watchtowers on its perimeter, erected to watch for body-snatchers or 'resurrectionists'. There was a thriving trade in bodies for medical schools in the first half of the 19th century. Visit the excellent museum for more detail on this gruesome trade (p.80).

Graveyard at Drumcondra Church. (Off Drumcondra Rd, turn right at the Cat and Cage pub, up Church Avenue). This is a quiet little churchyard. A report of 1831 lamented that no sooner was a body buried in this graveyard than it was removed by body-snatchers. A cottage was then provided for a watchman to watch over the graves. In the lee of the church is a fine early-19th-century mortsafe (an iron cage around the grave to keep away grave-robbers). Here also you can see James Gandon's grave (p.50).

Emmet's Execution. At St Catherine's Church in Thomas St is a modest plinth which commemorates the execution of the Irish patriot Robert Emmet. In 1803, Emmet led an abortive rebellion against British rule. After his capture and trial, he was hung and beheaded here before a large crowd in September 1803.

St Michan's Church. If you want an early intimation of your mortality, visit here. (Church St, D7, Tours €3, ☎ *01 8724154)*. The church dates from 1095 and was rebuilt in 1685. It is said that Handel practised at the organ here before his

Mummies of St Michan's

Messiah gig. Below the church are burial vaults. Here, due to limestone walls and a dry atmosphere, centuries-old bodies remain in a remarkable state of preservation. You can take a tour in the vaults. In one you see the mummified bodies, including one of a reputed Crusader who had to be sawn in half to fit into the coffin. Entering another vault, you can see the coffins of the Sheares brothers, executed in a gruesome manner after the 1798 rising. You can see why it is said that **Bram Stoker,** author of Dracula, gained inspiration for his novel here.

Surprisingly, there is not much to see in Dublin on Stoker. Born in 1847 at Marino Crescent, in Clontarf, he later studied at Trinity College. There is a plaque at 30 Kildare St, where he once lived.

Dubliner **Sheridan le Fanu** (1814-1873) was well known during the Victorian era as a writer of Gothick novels and was a leading proponent of the horror genre. Amongst his many works was *Carmilla*, a tale of a seductive and lesbian vampire. This helped inspire a clutch (or a 'bite'?) of vampire films. One of his stories, *Uncle Silas,* was made into a film and later remade as the *Dark Angel* with Peter O'Toole. You can see a plaque at 70, Merrion Square, where he lived. On a foggy morning go and see his grave at the suitably atmospheric Mount Jerome (p.81).

If you have strong nerves, take the **Dublin Bus Ghost Tour.** It transports you back to gas-lit Dublin, past haunted places, with the intention of shocking you on the way. The double-decker bus is in effect a mobile theatre, decorated in the gothic style. The task of the on-board storyteller is to charm, chill, and scare you with tales of ghosts, phantoms and derring-do. There are yarns about 'Black Jack Fitzgerald', 'Blind Igor, the Phibsboro Psychopath', 'Billy the Bowl of Stoneybatter' and many others. Costs €28, two hours. Mon-Thur 8pm; Fri-Sun 7pm & 9.30pm. Depart from Dublin Bus, 59 Upper O'Connell St, D1. *www.dublinsightseeing.ie.* ☎ *01 7033028.*

The Gravedigger Ghost Bus Tour takes you back 600 years to plague-ravaged Dublin. Professional actor-guides tell you legends and ghost stories whilst showing the scariest places in Dublin, including St Audeon's, Kilmainham Gaol, Bully's Acre, the Gravediggers Pub and the Black Church. Leaves College Green Tourism Office, D2, nightly at 7.45pm. Costs €25, two hours. *www.thegravedigger.ie.* ☎ *086 4113326.*

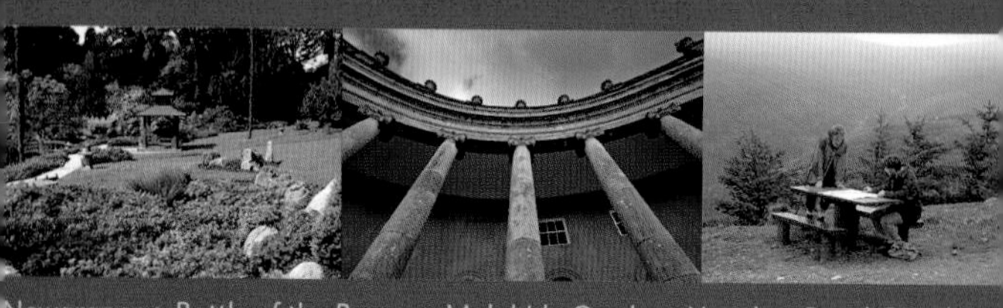

Newgrange • Battle of the Boyne • Malahide Castle • Howth • Royal Canal Wa
Wicklow Mountains • Newgrange • Battle of the Boyne • Malahide Castle • Hov
House • Hike in the Wicklow Mountains • Newgrange • Battle of the Boyne • M
scourt • Russborough House • Hike in the Wicklow Mountains • Newgrange • B
Glendalough • Powerscourt • Russborough House • Hike in the Wicklow Mount
Castletown House • Glendalough • Powerscourt • Russborough House • Hike i
• Royal Canal Walk • Castletown House • Glendalough • Powerscourt • Russb

Near Dublin

0 Places Within an Hour of Dublin

etown House • Glendalough • Powerscourt • Russborough House • Hike in the
l Canal Walk • Castletown House • Glendalough • Powerscourt • Russborough
astle • Howth • Royal Canal Walk • Castletown House • Glendalough • Power-
e Boyne • Malahide Castle • Howth • Royal Canal Walk • Castletown House •
wgrange • Battle of the Boyne • Malahide Castle • Howth • Royal Canal Walk •
klow Mountains • Newgrange • Battle of the Boyne • Malahide Castle • Howth
ouse • Hike in the Wicklow Mountains • Newgrange • Russborough House

There are many interesting things to visit and do near Dublin. Here are 10 of the best. Many are included in bus tours. Others are best reached by car. With a car you can combine visits: for example Newgrange with the Battle of the Boyne site, or Powerscourt and Glendalough.

Newgrange

Newgrange burial mound

The Boyne Valley has it all: fertile soil, land rolling down to a river with easy access to the sea. It is no wonder that this area is reputed to contain more Neolithic remains than anywhere else. There is more megalithic art in this valley than in Britain, France and Spain combined. The principal examples are the passage tomb mounds of Newgrange, Knowth and Dowth (currently under excavation) in County Meath.

At around 5000 years old, the remains at Newgrange (a UNESCO World Heritage site) are over 500 years older than the Great Pyramid at Ghiza in Egypt and predate Stonehenge in England by a millennium. This mound, over 75m in diameter and 12m high, was a Neolithic ritual centre and contains a passage tomb. Set around the mound are large stones with examples of megalithic art. The chamber inside the mound is corbelled to an ingenious design which keeps it dry.

These Neolithic farmers-cum -astronomers incorporated a light-box above the entrance to the passage to the chamber. It is aligned so that on the winter

Left: Inner chamber, Newgrange; Right: Neolithic art with spiral design

solstice, the cremated bones of the dead were illuminated by a shaft of light from the rising sun, for 17 minutes. You have to win in a special lottery to get a place on 21 December. A dramatic point on the tour is when, in the inner chamber under the mound, the guide re-creates this effect and light penetrates the darkness. Also accessible here is the great mound at Knowth. This has two passages, and is surrounded by 18 smaller satellite mounds.

Access to Newgrange and Knowth is only via the Visitor Centre. Visitors are brought from here to the monuments by shuttle bus. The *Brú na Bóinne* Visitor Centre (the name means the'palace' or 'mansion' of the Boyne and refers to the area within the bend of the river) is located on the south bank of the river and sensitively blends in with the environment. The centre interprets the Neolithic monuments of Newgrange,

Donore, Drogheda, Co Meath ☎ *041 9880300*
www.worldheritageireland.ie/bru-na-boinne
Opening times:
Nov–Jan 9am-5pm; Feb–Apr (and Oct): 9.30am-5.30pm
May (and mid-end Sept): 9am-6.30pm; Jun-mid Sept: 9am-7pm
Admission: Tour (includes Newgrange, Knowth and exhibition) €11
Getting there: One hour north of Dublin. Take the N2 north via Ashbourne towards Slane. Turn right about 2km south of Slane.

Tumuli at Knowth

Knowth and Dowth. There is an audio-visual display (also available in Irish, French, German, Italian and Spanish), reconstructions of Neolithic life (including homes, dress, food, tools and weapons). Included is a full-scale replica of the chamber at Newgrange.

A bus tour can be a convenient way to see the sites from Dublin. These include: **Bus Éireann's** day tour to *Brú na Bóinne*. The tour includes the exhibition and Newgrange tour, as well the Hill of Tara (site of the dining hall of the Irish High Kings), €28. *www.buseireann.ie*; **Mary Gibbons Tours** for day tours to Newgrange and the Hill of Tara, €35. *www.newgrangetours.com.*

Burial chamber, Knowth

02 Battle of the Boyne

Exhibition at Visitor Centre

The Protestant King William of Orange defeated the Catholic King James here on the banks of the River Boyne, near Drogheda, on 11th July 1690. The battle is enthusiastically celebrated by Loyalists in Northern Ireland on the 'Twelfth'.

As the Williamite army headed south, James chose to use the Boyne as a defensive line. 50,000 soldiers and artillery fought it out here. The Williamite army forded the river and eventually routed the Jacobite army.

The battle was decisive in setting the course of European history. The British throne was at stake, as well as issues such as the balance of religious power in Ireland and the wider one of French dominance among the European powers.

The Battle of the Boyne visitor centre (Oldbridge House) is well designed and helps to understand the momentous events that occurred here.
It is set near the river in pleasant pastoral and wooded surroundings.

You can take self-guided walks through the parkland and battle site (a map can be downloaded from the website). In the visitor centre there is an audio-visual display and a laser-assisted battlefield model. Original and replica 17th-century weapons are on display.

Visitor Centre

Oldbridge, Drogheda, Co Meath
☎ *041 9809950*
www.battleoftheboyne.ie

Opening times:
Daily. Mar-Apr: 9.30am-5.30 pm; May-Sept 10am-6pm;
Oct-Feb 9am-5.00 pm

Admission: €4

Getting there: Located on the south bank of the River Boyne, 3km north of Donore Village. Exit 9 (Slane/Drogheda) from the M1, then off N51.

In 1174 when the Anglo-Norman King Henry II came to Ireland he granted the lands and harbour of Malahide to his knight, Richard Talbot. The castle has been home for the Talbots over the centuries since.

There was a temporary problem when it was seized by the Cromwellians and awarded to one Miles Corbett, who was rewarded for being one of those who signed the death-warrant of Charles I. This Roundhead was later hanged and the castle was returned to the Talbots.

The family was on the losing Jacobite side at the Battle of the Boyne in 1690. Fourteen members of the Talbot family had breakfast in the Great Hall the morning before the battle, but all were dead by the evening of the next day.

Oak Room

The building was greatly enlarged in the 15th century, with the towers being added in 1765. Many historic castles and houses claim a ghost, but Malahide Castle tops the lot with five (including the Roundhead that was hanged).

Visit here to see how an aristocratic family lived. There is an exquisite collection of mid-18th century furniture as well as fine plasterwork. The Oak Room is stunning. The parkland of over 100 hectares, is a pleasant place to stroll. A new restaurant is due to open here in summer 2012.

Malahide Castle is part of the Dublin Bus North Coast tour. *www.dublinbus.ie*

Malahide Castle Demesne, Co Dublin

The castle is set to re-open in June 2012. Check *www.malahidecastleandgardens.ie* for opening hours.

Getting there: 14km north-east of Dublin.

Bus: 42 from Talbot Street.
DART: 10 minutes' walk from Malahide railway station

Howth

Ireland's Eye behind Howth Harbour and Lighthouse

How about visiting a pleasant village on a peninsula with a lovely harbour, overlooked by a heather-clad hill? That's Howth, easily accessible from Dublin.

King George IV came ashore here in 1821 on his visit to Ireland. He was reportedly drunk and in good humour, having heard of the death of his wife. The footprints where he stepped ashore have been carved into the stone of the quay and can still be seen near the end of the West Pier.

This is a working harbour and trawlers line the busy quayside. There is a continuous bustle as fish is landed, boats provisioned and nets mended. A family of grey seals have made their home in the harbour, recycling any spare fish. Fish, fresh from the quayside, is the speciality of the various restaurants and eateries along the quayside.

There are good views of Ireland's Eye and further north, Lambay Island. (There's an occasional ferry to Ireland's Eye. ☎*086 8459154*). The Howth Harbour lighthouse is at the end of the East Pier.

For an exhilarating walk along the cliffs of Howth Head, walk east along the Harbour Rd and then Balscadden Rd. The cliff walk leads to the Baily lighthouse from where there are superb views of Dublin Bay and the Wicklow Mountains.

Howth Castle is at the entrance to the village, with the National Transport Museum in its grounds. Crammed into a shed is a historic collection of old buses, trucks and trams (the last of which ran to here in 1959). *www.nationaltransportmuseum.org*.

A visit to Howth is included in the Dublin Bus North Coast tour. *www.dublinbus.ie*

Getting there: Howth is about 15 km northeast of Dublin.

Bus: 31, 31C. **Train:** 20 minutes by DART to Howth Station.

Pike Bridge Harbour

The Royal Canal was completed in 1817. Looping around to its north, it connected Dublin to the great River Shannon. However, it never captured much traffic from its southern rival, the Grand Canal. In 1845, it was taken over by the Midland Great Western Railway, which used the canal bank to build its line to the west. The canals were never able to compete with the railways, and traffic tailed off.

To sample this unique heritage you can walk along the canal from Leixlip to Maynooth (a little over 5km). This takes around 1½ hours, on flat terrain. Bring good walking shoes as it is muddy in parts.

Start westwards on the towpath from Louisa Bridge Station. (Check out the remains of the Leixlip Spa before you set out, it is signposted). As you walk, trains run on the other side of the canal. The first 10 minutes is suburban sprawl. Passing under the modern road-bridge you notice the Intel plant to the right, where the chips are silicon. After this it is peaceful, lined by trees, with water-birds, including swans and ducks. You pass Deey Bridge at the 13th lock and continue to Pike Bridge Harbour. You see the entrance to the 18th-century Carton House, once served by barges stopping at the quay here. Continuing on, eventually passing under a bridge, you reach the harbour in Maynooth. A pleasant university town, it is worth exploring, with several good cafés.

Location: About 16km west of Dublin.

Getting there and back: Train from Connolly Station to Leixlip (Louisa Bridge) Station. Return to Dublin by train from Maynooth Station. (or by bus No 66).

Castletown House

Castletown House

Castletown House has all the superlatives: the earliest, largest and finest Palladian mansion in Ireland.

It was built in1722-29 for William Conolly, speaker of the Irish House of Commons. The facade was designed by the Italian architect Alessandro Galilei, with additional wings by the Irishman Sir Edward Lovett Pearce. This house is one of the most important in terms of Ireland's and Europe's architectural heritage. It is now in State ownership and has been extensively renovated.

Conolly was born of humble origins in 1662 and eventually became a lawyer.

Entrance Hall

In the period after the defeat of James II in 1690, William of Orange confiscated the lands of James' supporters in Ireland. This proved to be Conolly's opportunity and he rapidly bought up forfeited lands. He built up a large land holding for relatively little and became fabulously wealthy. On his death he owned around 60,000 hectares.

Access to the house is by guided tour. It covers the history of Castletown House and tells the story of the Conolly family members who lived here. You can see the fine rooms, original furniture and collection of paintings throughout the house.
Come here to see exquisite plasterwork (by the Lafranchini brothers, creators of many of the finest ceilings of Georgian Dublin) in these grand surroundings.

The Entrance Hall is two

Long Gallery

storeys high and gives a foretaste of the grandeur of the house. Conolly insisted that Irish materials be used where possible, as is evident in the chequered floor of Kilkenny marble. One curiosity is the marble bust of George Washington (late 18th century). It was purchased to show Conolly's sympathy for the colonists during the American War of Independence. During the tour, you see boudoirs, bedrooms, dining rooms and several drawing rooms.

The Print Room, with a multitude of prints, shows the fashion of the late 18th century. It was the custom for ladies to collect their favourite prints, cut out parts of them and paste them on to the walls of a chosen room.

The Long Gallery is particularly impressive. It became a space for informal entertaining, including theatrical performances, often involving members of the family. Classical marble statues and busts are on display. In pride of place are the three Murano chandeliers, specially imported from Venice in 1770. With delicate colouring, these are beautiful and altogether exceptional.

Celbridge, Co Kildare
☎ *01 6288252*
www.castletownhouse.ie

Opening times:
Apr-Oct: Tues-Sun 10am-4.45pm

Admission: €4.50

Getting there: 20km from Dublin on the M4. Take the R449 Celbridge West/Leixlip West Exit 6, stay in the left hand lane and at the top of this slip road, at the roundabout take the first lane on the left. After around 100m you will see the Castletown Estate gates on the right.

Bus: 67 from Merrion Square to Celbridge and walk (15mins) up the avenue to the House.

Glendalough

View eastwards from Van Diemen's Land, to the Miners' Road

In Glendalough lived an auld saint
Renowned for his learning and piety

This is the start of a rather ribald song. But it is true: St Kevin founded an ecclesiastical settlement here in the 6th century.

Glendalough (*Gleann Dá Loch* or valley of the two lakes) offers an opportunity to see, not far from Dublin, a spectacular wooded valley and mountains, embracing some of Ireland's most impressive monastic remains. During the ice age, glaciers carved out the U-shaped valley and two lakes were formed as the ice thawed. The area is now the Wicklow Mountains National Park. The Visitor Centre has a good audio-visual show. You can book a guided tour of the monastic city in advance (available in many languages).

Go west along the green road and you reach the graveyard with the main monastic remains. Prominent among them is the round tower, 30m high. These could be bell towers or store-houses, but they were also places of refuge. Useful when the Vikings were raiding (as they did on three occasions). Among the buildings clustered around here are two churches from

Left: Monastic Settlement; Right: Upper Lake

the 12th century, as well as a 7th-century granite cross. The cathedral, dating from the 9th century, is in a central location. The church known as St Kevin's Kitchen dates from around the same era. This has a vaulted stone roof with a small tower projecting from it.

Continue on the walkway past the Lower Lake. In due course you arrive at the Upper Lake, spectacular under the brooding cliffs. It is a good place to linger and enjoy the views. You can examine the remains of an old stone fort and stone crosses. The Wicklow National Park Information office has useful information on the park.

St Kevin's Kitchen

Glendalough, Co Wicklow
☎*0404 45352*

Visitor Centre opening times:

Mid Oct-mid Mar: daily 9.30am-5pm

Mid Mar-mid Oct: daily 9.30am-6pm

Admission: €3

Getting there: M11/N11 to south. At Kilmacanogue take exit Roundwood/Glendalough (R755). Continue to Roundwood, Laragh and onto Glendalough .

Bus: St Kevin's Bus Service. ☎*01 2818119 www.glendaloughbus.com.* Return fare: €20

You can buy a map *The Walking Trails of Glendalough* at the Visitor Centre or the National Park Information Office. Caution: never ascend from here without walking boots and suitable clothing.

A good introductory walk is to take the **Miners' Road,** 5km in total. This skirts the north side of the Upper Lake, through Scots pine woodland. Halfway along you can just about make out, across the lake, the cave known as St Kevin's Bed. Eventually you come to an old mining village. Mining was carried out here from the 1790s and continued up to the 1920s. No vegetation grows in the mine waste due to the residues from the lead ore. The mines are overshadowed by the masses of granite scree on the northern slopes. The goats, common here and now feral, were introduced to provide milk for the miners.

Retrace your steps, or you can add an ascent up the zig-zag track with the cascading Glenealo river alongside, to catch great views of the lake or also of the bare higher valley, called Van Diemen's Land.

Other details of walks are on *www.walkinginireland.org/glendalough-walks.*

Powerscourt

Powerscourt House and lake

The Powerscourt estate is set in one of the most beautiful parts of Wicklow. In 1300, the Norman le Poer (Power) family built a castle here – from which the name Powerscourt derives. Many owners later, during the 1730s, the shell of the castle was remodelled, to form a magnificent mansion in Palladian style. The architect was the German-born Richard Cassels, (who also designed Leinster House and Russborough - next page). The Powerscourt Townhouse, in Dublin, was the city residence (1774) of Viscount Powerscourt.

In the 19th century the architect Daniel Robinson laid out the terraces, in an Italianate style. The story runs that Robinson, suffering from gout, directed operations from a wheelbarrow, equipped with a bottle of sherry. Be that as it may, the results are splendid.

Particularly fine is the southern vista to the conical Sugarloaf mountain. In front of the house you will find the marvellous Italian garden with the Triton Lake, overlooked by winged horses. There's a Dolphin Pond as well as a Japanese garden and a walled garden.

The house burnt down in 1974 and has been restored, with some property development on the estate (housing, golf course, luxury hotel) along the way. There is an Avoca store and in the Terrace Café you have good views of the Sugarloaf.

Many films have been made in the grounds including: *Barry Lyndon, David Copperfield, Excalibur* and the 2002 *Count of Monte Cristo.*

If you have a car, you can also visit the Powerscourt Waterfall, about 5km from the gardens. The waterfall, Ireland's highest, is in a spectacular valley of ancient trees.

Bus Éireann operates a day tour to Glendalough, Powerscourt Gardens and Wicklow. *www.buseireann.ie*

Enniskerry, Co Wicklow
☎ *01 2046000*
www.powerscourt.ie
Gardens opening times:
Daily 9.30am-5.30pm
Admission: €8
Getting there: M11/N11 to south, take exit for Enniskerry.
Bus: 44, 185 to Enniskerry. About 15 minutes walk to estate.

Russborough House

Russborough House is located in the scenic Wicklow countryside and has been described as the most beautiful house in Ireland.

The Palladian architectural style was embraced with enthusiasm by the great lords of Georgian Ireland for their mansions and townhouses. One of the most prominent 18th-century architects, Richard Cassels, used this style in his design of this fine house, completed in 1741, for John Leeson, who later became the Earl of Milltown.

Access to the building is by tour where you can explore the opulent rooms, with unique collections of silverware, porcelain, tapestries and furniture. There is Cuban and Santo Domingo mahogany. The outstanding baroque plasterwork is attributed to the Italian Lafranchini brothers. You can also visit a maze and an interactive exhibition. There is a walking route which allows you to see the demesne.

The house was bought by Sir Alfred Beit (whose wealth came from mining in South Africa) in 1952. His private collection of paintings was among the world's finest and most valuable – which attracted several thieves. The paintings stolen in a 1974 robbery were soon recovered. Most of those taken in 1986 by a criminal, known as the 'General', were also recovered. Some are on display here and the others are now in the National Gallery of Ireland in Dublin (p.22).

Blessington, Co Wicklow
☏*045 865239*
www.russborough.ie

Opening times:
May–Sept: daily 10am-6pm
April & Oct: Sun 10am-6pm

Admission: €9

Getting there: From Dublin, take the Tallaght (N81) exit off the M50, then drive for about 25 minutes along the N81. Pass Blessington village and continue south for around 3km.

10 Hike in the Wicklow Mountains

Ascent to a snowy Lugnaquilla, the highest mountain in Leinster

Dublin is fortunate to have Wicklow (called the 'Garden of Ireland') to its immediate south – the scenery here is among the best in Ireland. The granite mountains here, wooded or heather-clad, form the largest continous upland area in Ireland. There is a series of dramatic glaciated valleys, many lakes and wildlife, including deer.

Footfalls Walking Holidays, locally-based, offer a variety of walks in Wicklow and elsewhere. ☎*0404 45152. www.walkinghikingireland.com*.

For shorter trips: **Day Tours of Wicklow**. Bus tour to Wicklow (Mar-Sep) with opportunities for activities like hill-walking, horse-riding or mountain biking. ☎*087 7849599 www.daytours wicklow.ie*; **Walkabout Wicklow**. This is a bus tour, which includes a three to four-hour guided hike. Unsurprisingly, 'wet weather clothing is provided on request'. ☎*086 7929579 www.walkaboutwicklow.com.*

An excellent way to see Wicklow *profonde* is to buy the guide (see *www. wicklowway.com)*, and set out on the **Wicklow Way**, a 130km waymarked way from Dublin through the mountains. Start at Marlay Park, in Rathfarnham (Bus 16, 16A) and finish in Clonegal, Co Carlow, seven or eight days later, staying in B&Bs. The trek is moderate to hard, with highest altitudes around 400m, but including some isolated sections. The best time to do this is May-Sept. It can also be sampled as a shorter section (one day, as far as Glencree). Caution: to do this, you must be fit and able to navigate. Suitable boots and clothing are neccessary.

Listings

GETTING FROM THE AIRPORT

Taxis are expensive – around €20-30 to the city centre. Makes sense if you are in a hurry, or in a group of up to four.
Aircoach: Frequent coaches. At Terminal 1 (T1), turn left immediately as you exit the terminal building. At T2, continue along the same level, following the signs for buses, cross the footbridge, and exit down the escalator on the left hand side, over the bridge, outside the arrivals hall. Buses serve a variety of routes including the south city, via the centre. €7, return €12.
Airlink (Dublin Bus): Also outside T1 & 2, the 747 bus goes to a wide range of city-centre locations. €6, return €10.

GETTING AROUND IN THE CITY

Taxis

Taxis have a distinctive roof sign and can be hailed on the street or at taxi stands. Cars can take a maximum of four passengers, vans more. Taxis are regulated – it's not a free market on fares and the result is that these are expensive. Brace yourself: the starting cost is €4.10 (which covers the first kilometre) during the day or €4.45 at night or Sundays. Then you pay €1.03 (day) or €1.35 (night) per kilometre (plus extras, like €1 for a second and additional passenger). Solution: take public transport when you can.

Dublin Bus

Dublin Bus has an extensive network radiating from the city centre. *www.dublinbus.ie.* (also *dublin bus* App). Buses are frequent, and outside of rush-hour, reliable. Many stops have a useful display indicating the time of buses due. You have to pay the bus driver as you board. Cash fares range from €1.40 to €4.10 for a single journey. Have the exact fare, because if you insert more in the fare box, you do not get change, only a ticket to claim a refund from the Dublin Bus HQ. For convenience and flexibility, get a Leap Card (see below).

Luas

Glide to the centre of the city in comfort on *Luas* light rail. (*Luas* is 'speed' in the Irish language). *www.luas.ie* There are two networks: the Red Line runs southwest from Connolly or the Point (where the O2 is located) to Tallaght or Saggart; the Green Line runs southeast from St Stephen's Green to Sandyford and Bride's Glen. Trams operate from early morning to late evening at up to three minutes' frequency at peak and every10-20 minutes off peak. Tickets are available from machines at each stop. For convenience, get a Leap Card (see below).

DART

Beloved of Dubliners, the Dublin Area Rapid Transit system (DART), is a heavy-rail service that runs from the north (Malahide and Howth) to the south, mainly along the coast, to Bray and Greystones. There are also commuter rail services from Connolly to Maynooth, and from Heuston to Hazelhatch. Tickets can be bought at stations. For convenience, get a Leap card (see below). *www.irishrail.ie*

Leap Card

If you are in the city for a few days, it makes sense to get a Leap Card. This is valid on all public transport in the city: Dublin Bus, *Luas*, DART and commuter rail services. Fares using the card are cheaper than when paying cash on DART, Luas etc. It also means no more rooting around for change or queuing at ticket machines. You can buy or put credit on a card at over 400 ticket agents around the city, see *www.leap.ie* for locations. There is a refundable deposit of €5, with minimum top-up of €5 travel credit.

TRAVEL AROUND IRELAND

Railway

Iarnród Éireann (Irish Rail) operates trains around the Republic of Ireland. The network radiates from Dublin. Flagship services are on the routes Dublin-Belfast and Dublin-Cork (where you can travel at

speeds up to 160km/hr). Following a big investment programme, trains are very modern and comfortable. Tickets can be purchased at stations, but best to book online for special low-cost fares. *www. irishrail.ie.* Trains from Dublin usually take the following times: Cork – 2hr 45min; Belfast – 2hr 15min; Waterford – 2hr 25min; Limerick – 2hr 15min; Galway – 2hr 40min; Killarney – 3hr 25min.
The main Dublin stations are: Heuston Station (trains to Cork, Waterford, Kilkenny, Limerick, Galway, Tralee and Killarney); Connolly Station (trains to Belfast, Sligo, Mullingar and Wexford). *www.irishrail.ie.*

Bus Éireann

The website says 'travel anywhere in Ireland by bus or coach with Bus Éireann', and it does exactly what it says. The company operates a dense bus network (with modern comfortable buses) across the country. Buses depart from Busáras, the central bus station, on Store St. *www.buseireann.ie.*

Other Bus Operators

Those with scheduled services include: *www.jjkavanagh.ie* for services Dublin-Kilkenny-Waterford; *www.gobus.ie* for services Dublin-Galway; *www.matthews.ie* for services Dublin-Dundalk. Google the web for details of bus operators to other destinations.

ACCOMMODATION

The recession has driven Dublin hotel prices significantly down. If you choose accommodation out of the central area, check for a location with easy public transport links. Use Trip Advisor, *www. tripadvisor.com,* for a dynamically-updated take on the best accommodation in the city. Use it with caution, knowing that the comments and ratings can swing widely and are open to manipulation.

CAFÉS

Bewley's Café, 78/79 Grafton St, D2. ☏*01 6727720*. A Dublin institution. Large café, in grand surroundings.
Cake Café, Daintree Building, Pleasant's Place, D2. ☏*01 4789394*. A hidden delight – worth discovering. An excellent bakery and café, in the Daintree building, which stretches from Camden St to Pleasant's Place.
Queen of Tarts, Cork Hill, Dame St, D2 and another branch round the corner at Cow's Lane. ☏*01 633 4681*. Traditional tea-room, breakfast and lunch. Charming, high-class tarts of the sweet and savoury kind. Weekend brunch. Yum.
Tea Garden, 7 Lower Ormond Quay, D1. ☏*086 2191010*. This is not tea as mum used to make it. Come here, to this atmospheric place, with echoes of the Kasbah, to explore the delights of pu-erh, green tea and more.
Science Gallery Café, Pearse St (near corner of Westland Row). ☏*01 8964091*. One of Dublin's best lunch secrets. Good food for very little. It's an opportunity also to see the Science Gallery.
Cobalt Café, 16 North Great George's St. D1. ☏*01 8730313*. Eat in a bright, high-ceilinged room located in a grand Georgian house. Lively place for an appetising and good-value lunch. Sometimes they present plays and concerts.

RESTAURANTS

There was little fine dining in Dublin decades ago. Over the years the city has shaken itself from its gastronomic torpor and now there is good (even excellent!) cuisine to be had. On prices and value: regrettably, despite being in a deep recession, many Dublin restaurants still have not got it – they still charge excessive prices. Listed here are places with good value and tasty food, with a small selection also in the moderate range (phone in advance, check times and go for the early-bird menus). A few expensive places are listed, if you want to say 'hang the expense'.

Good Food, Great Value

Anderson's Creperie, 1a Carlingford Road, Drumcondra, D9. ☎*01 8305171*. Worth venturing north to sample excellent food, reasonable prices.The galettes are delicious. Open till 7pm (Fri 8pm). Jazz on some Wednesday evenings.

Boojum, Millennium Walkway, D1. Your fajita or burrito is made to your choice – tastes great, costs little. Small seating area. This Mex joint is hopping: big queues at lunchtime.

Honest to Goodness, 25 George's St Arcade, D2. Lively lunch place. Best value soup in Dublin. Flavoursome fresh food.

KC Peaches Café & Delicatessen. 28/29 Nassau St, D2. ☎*01 6336872*. Buzzy, good food at good prices. Open all day.

Keshk, 129 Upper Leeson St, D4. ☎01 6689793. Understated café, limited menu, but great-tasting food in Egyptian style.

Kimchi, 160-161 Parnell St, D1. ☎*01 8728318*. Good Korean and Japanese cuisine with friendly service. Parnell St in the north inner city is being developed as Dublin's Oriental Quarter.

M & L Szechuan Chinese Restaurant, 13-14 Cathedral St, D1. ☎*01 8748038*. This is as authentic as it gets. Just off O'Connell St, you could be dining down a side-street in Beijing. All around you Chinese patrons dig into tasty and good value food. Lunch/dinner.

Paulie's Pizza, 58 Upper Grand Canal St, D4. ☎*01 664 3658*. At last a Dublin pizza house that can match those in Italy. Dinner.

Terra Madre, 13A Bachelor's Walk, D1. Tiny basement café. Short menu. Authentic Italian food for a few euros. Lunch/dinner.

Ukiyo, 7-9 Exchequer St, D2. ☎*01 6334071*. Japanese with Korean fusion. Modern, understated décor. Delicious food. Lunch/dinner.

Urban Picnic, 30-31 George's St Arcade, D2. ☎*087 9775822*. Simple place offering a tasty lunch.

Medium Expensive

Coppinger Row, off South William St, D2. ☎*01 6729884*. Mediterranean. Worth trying the *menú del día* lunch offer. Lunch/ dinner.

Dunne and Crescenzi, 14-16 South Frederick St, D2. ☎*01*

6759892. Atmospheric restaurant in central location. Flavoursome and authentic Italian food. Lunch/dinner.
Eden, Meeting House Square, Temple Bar, D2. ☎*01 6705372.* Contemporary Irish food in a minimalist setting. Lunch/dinner.
La Cave Wine Bar, 28 Sth Anne St, D2. ☎*01 6794409.* Good affordable food in what could be a Paris bistro. Lunch/dinner.
Les Frères Jacques, 74 Dame St, D2. ☎*01 6794555.* Authentic French cuisine. Mid-week menu offers value. Lunch/dinner.
Juno's Café, 26 Parkgate St, D8. ☎*01 6709820.* Go west, young diner! Small, but perfectly formed restaurant producing good food, near Heuston Station and Phoenix Park (Museum stop on the Luas Red Line). Lunch/dinner.
Pichet, 14-15 Trinity St, D2. ☎*01 6771060.* Good food on a French theme. Lunch/dinner.
Rigby's, 126 Upper Leeson St, D2. ☎*087 7939195.* Diner by day, dinner at night. Simple, no menu. Bring your own bottle (BYOB).
Tea Rooms, The Clarence, 6-8 Wellington Quay, D2. ☎*01 4070813.* Good food in an elegant former ballroom with a soaring ceiling. Lunch/dinner.

Haute Cuisine/Michelin – Blow the Wallet

Chapter One, Basement of Writers' Museum, 18-19 Parnell Square, D1. ☎*01 8732266.* Michelin star. Interesting range of menus. Queen Elizabeth II dined here in 2011.
L'Écrivain, 109a Lower Baggot St, D2. ☎*01 6611919.* Michelin star. Good food in former Georgian coach house, with the usual small portions.
Restaurant Patrick Guilbaud, 21 Upper Merrion St, D2. ☎*01 6764192.* Ireland's only two-star Michelin, with Gallic flair.

Southern Delights

There's excellent value from the middle of Camden St (a street with echoes of the Lower East Side) to Rathmines Rd. Heading south:
Neon, 17 Camden St, D2. ☎*01 4052222.* Intelligently re-imagines the street food of Hanoi. Worth a visit. Lunch/dinner.
Green 19, 19 Camden St Lower, D2. ☎*01 4789626.* Main courses

at €10. Top notch nosh. Good food and one of the best value restaurants in Dublin. Lunch/dinner.
The Bernard Shaw, 11-12 South Richmond St, D2. ☎*085 712 8342*. Real Italian coffee in the morning, terrific Abruzzo cuisine for lunch (great *arrosticini*, lamb on skewers) at delightfully low prices (8am-6.30pm). BYOB at lunchtime. Observe works of high-end graffiti artists on the adjacent hoardings outside.
Seagrass, 30 South Richmond St, D2. ☎*01 4789595*. Good quality food in Irish-continental mode. Reasonable early-bird and lunch prices. Lunch/dinner.
Rotana, 31 South Richmond St, D2. ☎*01 4759969*. Lebanese cuisine, with falafel, home-made baklawa and more. Shisha (hubble bubbles to you and me) are available for the outside table with flavours such as apple or strawberry. BYOB. Lunch/dinner.
Lennox Café Bistro, 31 Lennox St, D8. ☎*01 4789966.* Appetising food, New York cool. Good breakfast and lunch menu.
Little Jerusalem, 3 Wynnfield Rd, Rathmines, D6. ☎*01 4126912.* On a side street off Rathmines Rd Lower, a great Palestinian restaurant, good food. Also serve kosher food. BYOB. Dinner.
Zen Restaurant, 89 Upper Rathmines Rd, D6. ☎*01 4979428.* In a former church, award-winning Szechuan food. Lunch/dinner.
161 Café and Bistro, 161 Upper Rathmines Rd, D6. ☎*01 4978049*. Classy joint. Worth travelling to the south city for the tasty early-bird deals. Lunch/dinner.

SHOPPING

Department Stores

Arnotts, 12 Henry Street, D1. Big, classic department store in a late-Victorian building.
Brown Thomas, 88-95 Grafton Street, D2. The most prestigious of them all. This store has been a fixture in Dublin since 1849. High-end, with high quality and prices to match.
Clerys, 18-27 Lower O'Connell St, D1. A Dublin institution, it was where the priests and nuns shopped in the past. There are many

floors, and now slick fashion franchises, in this central store.
Avoca, 11-13 Suffolk St, D2. Mini-department Store. Good to browse in. Has fashion, home furnishings, jewellery, kids' wear and toys. Coffee shop and food hall.

Shopping Centres

George's Street Arcade, South Great George's St, D2. Come here to see what a late-19th-century shopping arcade looks like. This arcade is set in a fantastical red-turreted building, with a touch of Ruritania. The Bohemian mix inside includes young clothing, jewellery, music, bookshops, collectables, souvenirs and cafés.
Jervis Shopping Centre, Henry St, D1. This modern mall is bounded at the western end by the remains of a former Victorian hospital. All the accoutrements of a mall are here: fashion and accessory shops, supermarkets and more.
Powerscourt Centre, 59 South William St, D2. This was the townhouse of Viscount Powerscourt (his other pad was his main residence, Powerscourt Estate in Co Wicklow, p.118) This is the elegant home of many stores, mainly catering for equally elegant young ladies. A Georgian 'Grand Tour' (€3.50) , starts from the South William St entrance (Thurs, Sat) at 11am and 2pm
St Stephen's Green Shopping Centre, St Stephen's Green West, D2. The architecture has been described as 'Mississippi Riverboat'. This late-1970s mall is bursting with over a hundred shops.
Westbury Mall, Harry St (off Grafton St, D2). Small mall, in the lee of the five-star Westbury Hotel. Upmarket jewellery and accessory shops. There are also jewellery shops along the adjoining alley between Grafton St and Clarendon St, Johnson's Court. For jewellery and watches at the high-quality and expensive end go to the long-established **Weir and Son**s, 96-99 Grafton St, D2.

Women's Clothes – High-End

Costume, 10 Castle Market, D2.
Helen McAlinden, 20, South William St, D2. Stylish elegance.
The Design Centre, Top Floor, Powerscourt Centre, 59 South William St, D2. Good range of Irish and international designers.

Vintage and Second-Hand Designer Shops

Déjà Vu, 4 Ranelagh Rd, Dublin 6 (opposite the Luas stop). Again a wide selection of designer clothes, but here the coy euphemism is to describe the stock as 'gently worn'.

Green with Envy, 302 Rathmines Rd Lower, D6. Located above the Boots Store, a fashion exchange and vintage boutique with the added touch of an art gallery.

Jenny Vander, 50 Drury St, D2. Fabulous. The grand dame of vintage shops: all ages, all prices.

Wear it Again, 147 Lower Baggot St, D2. This is an upscale place – come here to get what is coyly called a 'pre-loved' designer piece. That little black dress will cost you, but at less than the original price.

Vintage: Young

Harlequin, 13 Castle Market, D2. Cool, retro, vintage clothes, sunglasses, jewellery, leather bags and hats. Men's clothes in basement.

Lucy's Lounge, 11 Fownes St, D2. Modish vintage clothes and accessories, male and female, in the heart of Temple Bar. Enter here for an atmospheric, fun and innovative experience.

Om Diva, 27 Drury St, D2. Inside this red-brick Victorian building, are many stories of interesting clothing and associated things. Vintage clothes in the basement; contemporary on the ground floor. Head to the first floor for 'Atelier 21', showing the work of graduate designers.

9 Crow Street, Crow St, Temple Bar, D2. You can sell, consign or swap designer clothing, shoes and accessories.

Bookshops

Lots of excellent bookshops in this lively and literary city:

Alan Hanna's Bookshop, 270 Rathmines Rd Lower, D6. All the latest books are here and it specialises in Irish books.

Books on the Green, 2 Seafort Avenue, Sandymount Village, D4. Small bookshop with the latest books and a well-chosen selection.

Books Upstairs, 36 College Green, D2. Convenient city-centre location, just across the road from Trinity College. Good selection of Irish literature and history. A great place to browse.
Cathach Books, 10 Duke St, D2. Maps and prints, antiquarian books. Signed copies and rare editions.
Chapters, Parnell St, D1. Two floors with a huge range of books, music and DVDs, both new and secondhand. The best selection of bargain-priced titles in Dublin, worth a journey.
The Company of Books, 96 Ranelagh Village, D6. Cool bookshop in affluent suburb.
Dubray Books, 36 Grafton St, D2. Three floors of books, a good selection in this central location. (Other central branches are in the Hugh Lane Gallery, Parnell Square and the Swan Centre, Rathmines).
Eason, 40 Lower O'Connell St, D1. Huge store with books on many floors. Big collection of maps and guide books, Irish and foreign. A wide selection of magazines from the commonplace to the esoteric. A Tower Records branch is on the second floor. (Other branches at the Irish Life Centre, Talbot St; Busáras and Heuston Station.)
The Gutter Bookshop, Cow's Lane, D2. Elegant bookshop, in the heart of the interesting Cow's Lane quarter of (western) Temple Bar.
Hodges Figgis, 56-58 Dawson St, D2. Established in the 18th century, this is Dublin's serious book shop. Large, with three floors and basement, take the many stairs to book heaven. Great range, including a large selection of Irish interest.
Hughes and Hughes, Ground Floor, St Stephen's Green Shopping Centre, D2. Central location.
Rathgar Bookshop, 100 Rathgar Rd, D6. Small bookshop with excellent selection, also a 'Little Coffee Shop' for a coffee.
Reads, 24-26 Nassau St, D2. Good range of books (fiction and non-fiction) at discounted prices. Also magazines, gifts and stationery.
The Winding Stairs, 40, Ormond Quay, D1. New and second-hand. Irish books as well as the classics. You can have a cup of real coffee here. Restaurant upstairs for fine dining.

CD Stores

Tower Records. 6-8 Wicklow St, D2, also third floor at Eason's, O'Connell St. Biggest selection in Dublin. CDs, DVDs, plus the usual books, games and T-shirts.
Celtic Note, 14-15 Nassau St, D2. Selection of Irish & roots music.
Claddagh Records, 2 Cecilia St, Temple Bar, D2. The best selection of Irish traditional music around. Mail order on *www.claddaghrecords.com*.
HMV, 65 Grafton St, D2. Chain store with CDs, DVDs, videos and video games.

Second-Hand CDs

Lots around Temple Bar and its neighbourhood:
E2Music, College Green, D2. Music and DVD shop that buys and sells CDs, also new CDs and DVDs. Well organised, good prices.
Mojos Records. 4, Merchant's Arch, Temple Bar, D2, Tiny. New and second-hand CDs, DVDs, with an emphasis on Irish. Also books.
R.A.G.E. Records, 16b Fade St, D2. Games and huge selection of second-hand vinyl.
Spindizzy, George's St Arcade, D2. New and second-hand, all genres.
The Secret Book & Record Store, 15a Wicklow St, D2. Easy to miss, reached along a corridor. Extensive selection of second-hand CDs and books.
Trout Records, George's St Arcade, D2. Good selection of second-hand CDs, all genres.

Crafts & Souvenirs

Carroll's Gifts and Souvenirs. This is souvenir central. Come here to this well-organised store if you want that leprechaun costume or Viking hat. There's lot more besides, like Guinness rugby shirts, glassware and a myriad other things. Ubiquitous, with stores all over central Dublin: Westmoreland St; O'Connell St, Talbot St; Henry St; Suffolk St; St Stephen's Green Shopping Centre.

Kilkenny, 6-15 Nassau St, D2. A large store with Irish-designed contemporary crafts.
The Sweater Shop, 9 Wicklow St, D2. In the 1960s a traditional singing group called the Clancy Brothers wore white woolly Aran sweaters. You can get these here, as well as conventional fare.
Dublin Woollen Mills. By the Ha'penny Bridge. Long-established (James Joyce acted as their agent in Trieste from 1906 to 1911) shop selling Irish knitwear.

Markets

Art & Crafts Market, first Sunday of every month. The Coop, Newmarket Square (off Cork St), D8. Also in the same location:
Dublin Flea Market, last Sunday of every month. Ranges from clothes to books and records. Great bargains. Indoor and outdoor stalls.
Designer Mart, Cow's Lane, Temple Bar, D2. This outdoor market (handmade arts and design) is located in the Old City (western) area of Temple Bar. Sat, 10am-5pm.
Ha'penny Flea Market, Grand Social, 35 Lower Liffey St, D1. Every Sat, 11am-5pm. Stalls with everything: crafts, vintage clothes, art, bargain books, DVDs and vinyl records.
Lunchtime Markets operate across the city (stalls offering a variety of Irish and international foods, jazz and other music): *Wed:* Jan-Dec 11.30am-2pm. Central Square, Spencer Dock, D1; EastPoint, EastPoint Business Park, D3. *Thurs*: Mespil Rd (on the banks of the Grand Canal), Mespil Rd, D4. Jan-Dec 11.30am-2pm; Christ Church, Christ Church Cathedral, D2. Mar-Dec 11.30am-2pm (and Sat); *Fri*: Carmanhall Rd, Sandyford Industrial Estate, D18. Jan-Dec 11am-2pm; Grand Canal, Percy Place, D4, Jan-Dec 11.30am-2pm; Fitzwilliam Square, D2. Apr-Dec 12 noon-2.30pm.
Merrion Square Art. Every weekend, the sides of this square are hung with art. Sat, Sun 10am-6pm. The quality ranges from the good to the bad and, occasionally, the ugly. Chat with the artists who are in attendance, bargain, and you may get that wonderful piece to hang on the wall.

Temple Bar Book Market, Temple Bar Square, Temple Bar, D2. Sat, Sun, 11am-6pm.

Temple Bar Food Market, Meeting House Square, Temple Bar, D2. Sat, 10am-4.30pm. With a good range, a foodie's paradise. Now under a retractable canopy.

Food and Drink

Avoca, 11-13 Suffolk St, D2. An extensive food hall on the ground floor, tasty stuff. (Café on the top floor).

The Bretzel, 1a Lennox St, Portobello, D8. Here you can get fresh (and kosher) croissants, bagels, sourdough and much more.

Celtic Whiskey Shop, 27-28 Dawson St, D2. You can taste Irish whiskies here and also compare with the extensive range of Scotch and world whiskies also in stock. (See p.46 for the Old Jameson Distillery tour).

Magills, 14 Clarendon St, D2. Low-key delicatessen. One of the best in the city.

Liston's Food Store, 25-26 Lr Camden St, D2. As they say, it is 'honest, healthy food'. Top quality.

Sheridan's Cheesemongers, 11 South Anne St, D2. Irish cheese has improved exponentially in recent decades. Visit here to check out the wide variety.

TOURS

1916 Rebellion Walking Tour. Tour visiting many of the places where this seminal event in Ireland's struggle for independence unfolded. Two hours. €12. ☏ *086 8583847*

Architecture Tours Ireland. Choice of walking tours including Georgian Dublin. ☏ *01 6761703*

City Bus Tours, in French, Italian, Spanish. Around 90 minutes, daily. €16. ☏ *01 4580054*.

Dublin City Bike Tours. They provide you with the use of a bike and helmet. Tours include: The *Dublin City Tour* covering the principal parts of the central city, led by a guide, takes 2-3 hours. €24. The *Downhill to Dublin,* plus coastal ride to Howth, takes a full

day and costs €70. You see it all: the Dublin/Wicklow mountains, south side suburbia, the Grand Canal, Docklands/city centre, Bull Island and the fishing village of Howth. There is transport to the starting point in the Dublin/Wicklow mountains and it includes a meal, snacks and a train ride back to the city. ☎ *087 1341866.*

City Sightseeing Bus Tour. 90-minute tour with departures daily every 8-15 minutes throughout the year. €6. ☎ *01 4580054.*

Dublin Bus Tours. A variety of tours including the classic 'hop on, hop off' bus tour. This has a live English commentary and pre-recorded multilingual commentary in 10 languages. Daily from 9am. Can be joined at any of 23 stops, an easy way to see the principal sights. €16. ☎ *01 7033028.*

Dublin City Pub-Crawl. Starts at 8pm. €12, including a pint. ☎ *086 4020040.*

Dublin Literary Pub-Crawl. Literature and alcohol, what a mix! A trip around selected pubs with actors performing the works of the best-known city writers. Evenings, around two hours. ☎ *01 6705602.*

Historical Walking Tours of Dublin. Two hours of Irish history, visiting some of the main locations in the city. ☎ *087 6889412.*

Hidden Dublin Walking Tours. A scary variety of ghost walks. ☎ *085 1023646.*

Ingenious Ireland. Something different: self-guided tours of Dublin for the discerning. Download from *www.ingeniousireland.ie*

Liffey River Cruises. Sail up the river through the heart of the city. Departures from boardwalk off Bachelor's Walk, about 100m west of O'Connell Bridge. €14. ☎ *01 4730000.*

Musical Pub-Crawl. Evening tours, two-and-a-half hours, visiting a selection of central pubs, with Irish music on tap. €12. ☎ *01 4753313.*

Pat Liddy's Walking Tours of Dublin. Pat Liddy is the author of several books on Dublin history. Many tours daily including: *Highlights and Hidden Corners*; *Viking and Medieval Dublin*; *Castle & Cathedral*. Prices range from €6 to €12. ☎ *0818205205.* Also **Tour in German,** *Stadtbesichtigung auf Deutsch. Samstags* 2pm, 37 College Green, Dublin 2. €12. *www.walkingtours.ie.*

Tours in Spanish. *Visita y explora Irlanda en español. Todos: Glendalough, Howth y Malahide; Tour histórico de Pubs; Tour de Dublin, dos horas,* €15. ☏*01 6678834.*
Sea Safari. Experience a sea tour of the Dublin Bay area, at high speed in a rib. About 90 minutes. From €35. ☏*01 6689802.*
Segway Tours. The *Segway Phoenix Park Tour*. This two-hour guided tour on a Segway is expensive at €50. The two-hour *Dublin Docklands Tour* also costs €50. ☏*01 8223388.*
Viking Splash Tours. Fun tour, great for kids. ☏*01 7076000*

MEDIA, MUSIC & LITERATURE

Newspapers

Serious newspapers, with content that will engage your mind:
Irish Times. Very broadsheet, never tabloid. The voice of the Protestant Ascendancy during the 19th century. Now a liberal and lively newspaper, enjoyed by the middle classes.
Irish Independent. Broadsheet, also in tabloid form. Centre-based paper. Good coverage, read by the plain people of Ireland.
Irish Examiner: This broadsheet is published in Cork and has a loyal Munster readership. Now a national newspaper.
Sunday Business Post. A little dull, but best Sunday.

Recommended CDs

Essential Chieftains (Sony Music). Mixed bag from this iconic group, with an electrifying *Foggy Dew* by Sinéad O'Connor.
Journey: Best of Donal Lunny (Grapevine). Seminal figure at the heart of great Irish music in the traditional vein. In this retrospective he appears with the greats including Sharon Shannon and Maighréad & Tríona Ní Dhomhnaill.
Masters of Irish Music, Frankie Gavin and Alec Finn (Shanachie). Traditional fiddle-playing at its best.
Ó Riada sa Gaiety (Gael Linn). Atmospheric 1970 concert of Irish traditional music, with a large band of talented musicians, in the Gaiety Theatre, directed by the pioneering Seán Ó Riada.
Planxty (Shanachie). Hugely influential, the beginning of modern

Irish folk. Planxty play music by the great composer Carolan and other classics.
Soldier of Fortune: The Best of Phil Lynott and Thin Lizzy (Telstar). Contains all the classics: *Whiskey in the Jar*, and *The Boys are Back in Town*.
Sult - Spirit of the Music (Hummingbird). Hopping cross-section of (genuine) Irish music by a variety of artists.
The Joshua Tree (Mercury). Classic U2, a CD with songs of real depth, produced by Daniel Lanois.

DVDs

Mise Éire. 1959 documentary on Ireland's War of Independence by the gifted George Morrison. Score by Seán Ó Riada.
Michael Collins. Fast-paced 1996 film by Neil Jordan on Ireland's lost leader (played by Liam Neeson).
The Best of Riverdance (1995). With Michael Flatley and Jean Butler, the original stars, this captures the energy of the first dance spectacle. It even established the idea that erotic tension and Irish dancing did not together amount to an oxymoron.
The Commitments (Dir. Alan Parker). A1991 slice of gritty (and pre-Celtic Tiger) Dublin. Best soul music east of the Atlantic.

Books on Dublin & Ireland

A Short History of Dublin, Richard Killeen, Gill & Macmillan 2010.
Bernard Shaw: A Biography, Michael Holroyd , Vintage, 1998.
Dublin 1916: The Siege of the GPO, Clair Wills, Profile Books, 2010.
Dublin Made Me, C.S. Andrews, The Lilliput Press, 2001
Dublin: The Fair City, Peter Somerville-Large, Sinclair-Stevenson, 1996
Exploring Georgian Dublin, Pat Dargan, History Press, 2008
Ireland: A History, Thomas Bartlett, Cambridge University Press, 2010
James Joyce's Dublin: A Topographical Guide to the Dublin of Ulysses, Clive Hart, Thames and Hudson, 2004.

Leisure Walks near Dublin, Joss Lynam, Gill & Macmillan, 2004
Oscar Wilde, Richard Ellmann, Penguin, 1998
Ulysses, James Joyce, Penguin Classics, 2000
Victorian Dublin Revealed, Michael Barry, Andalus Press, 2012
Walking Dublin: Twenty-four Original Walks, Pat Liddy, New Holland, 2004.

GENERAL INFORMATION

Banks, ATMs, Currency

Most banks change foreign currency. Banking hours are generally Mon-Fri 10am-4pm. ATMs are to be found in most locations. Ireland is in the Eurozone. Currently, the euro is king.

Cinemas

You can go and see a 'fillum' – as Dubliners pronounce 'film', (Here's the technical bit: it is insertion of the epenthetic vowel, a trait of Hiberno-English, of origin in the Irish language).
Some central cinemas:
IFC, 6 Eustace St, Temple Bar, D2. World cinema. *www.ifi.ie*
Lighthouse, Smithfield, D7. Intelligent arthouse in a sparkling new venue. *www.lighthousecinema.ie.*
Savoy, O'Connell Street, D1. Central, many screens. Claims to have 'Ireland's biggest screen'. *www.savoy.ie.*
Screen. D'Olier St, D2. Smaller cinema with several screens, sometimes adventurous choices. Check out the bronze usher at the front. *www.screencinema.ie.*
Cineworld, Parnell St, D1. Big cinema complex. *www.cineworld.ie.*

Dublin Festivals

Temple Bar Tradfest: January. Irish/roots music. *www. templebartrad.com*
Dublin International Film Festival: February. *www.jdiff.com*
St Patrick's Festival: events around St Patrick's Day on 17th March. *www.stpatricksfestival.ie*
Bloomsday: Events around 16 June, the day Leopold Bloom walked

around Dublin in Joyce's *Ulysses*. *www.jamesjoyce.ie*
Dublin Theatre Festival: October. www.*dublintheatrefestival.com*

Climate & When to Come

Dublin has a temperate Atlantic climate. It rarely gets very cold or hot, but the drawback is that there is frequent rain. Average daily range of temperature: January (3°-8°); April (4°-12°); July (12°-19°); September (10°-17°). Best months for a visit are from April to September. June has longest days, April is the driest month.

Electricity

Those curious three-square-pin plugs (IS411 or BS1363) are used, as in the UK. It is 230V, 50Hz.

Embassies

Australia, 7th Floor, Fitzwilton Hse, Wilton Tce, D2. ☎ *01 6645300.*
Belgium, 2 Shrewsbury Rd, Ballsbridge, D4. ☎ *01 2057100.*
Brazil, Harcourt Centre, Charlotte Way, D2. ☎ *01 4756000*
Canada, 3rd Floor, 7-8 Wilton Tce, D2. ☎ *01 2344000.*
China, 40 Ailesbury Rd, D4. *01 2691707*
Denmark, Block E, Iveagh Ct, Harcourt Rd, D2. ☎ *01 4756404.*
Egypt, Clyde Rd, Ballsbridge, D4. ☎ *01 6606566*
France, 36 Ailesbury Rd, D4. ☎ *01 2775000.*
Germany, 31 Trimleston Ave, Booterstown. ☎ *01 2693011.*
India, 6 Leeson Park, D6. ☎ *01 4966792.*
Italy 63-65 Northumberland Rd, Ballsbridge, D4. ☎ *01 6601744.*
Japan, Merrion Centre, Nutley Lane, D4. ☎ *01 2028300.*
Netherlands, 160 Merrion Rd, Ballsbridge, D4. ☎ *01 2693444.*
Poland, 5 Ailesbury Rd, Ballsbridge, D4. ☎ *01 2830855.*
Russia 184-186 Orwell Rd, Rathgar, D14. ☎ *01 4922048.*
Saudi Arabia, 6-7 Fitzwilliam Square East, D2. ☎ *01 6760704.*
Spain, 17A Merlyn Park, D4. ☎ *01 2839900.*
Switzerland, 6 Ailesbury Rd, Ballsbridge, D4. ☎ *01 2186382*
United Kingdom, 29 Merrion Rd, Ballsbridge, D4. ☎ *01 2053700.*
United States of America, 42 Elgin Rd, Ballsbridge, D4. ☎ *01 6306200.*

Event Listings

www.dublineventguide.com is a weekly events website. *www.visitdublin.ie* has news of events.There are many free listings sheets/magazines (*Totally Dublin* is good) available at most tourist locations. The *Irish Times* has *The Ticket* on Fridays with excellent listings. Also check the exuberant fly-posters around the city.

Internet

Central Internet Café, 6 Grafton St, D2. ☎*01 6778298.*
Global Internet Café, 8 Lower O'Connell St, D1. Good coffee and organic teas. Also has a left luggage service. ☎*01 8780295.*
Internet and Call Shop, 7 Eustace St, D2. ☎*01 6771301.*
Internet and Call Shop, 38 Dame St, D2. ☎*087 7782004*

Free WiFi in city parks and some streets, by Dublin City Council.

Mail

General Post Office. O'Connell St, D1. Come here for stamps, philately and history. The rising was centred here in 1916.
Andrew's St Post Office, 19-24 St Andrew's St, D2.

Maps

DCBA Map of Dublin is the best map for tourists: it is simple to read, with most tourist attractions shown. Available free at most tourist outlets and hotels all over the city.
Ordnance Survey of Ireland Maps: Good for maps of Ireland. The 1:50,000 series covering the entire country is excellent for hiking.

Public Libraries

Central libraries are at the ILAC Centre, Henry St, D1 and at 138-144 Pearse St, D2. Free internet access.

Safety

Dublin is as safe as most European cities. Most of the following states the obvious and is summed up as - use your common sense:

- Place passport and valuables in the safe in your hotel.
- Don't wear expensive jewellery or leave belongings exposed.
- Use a handbag or shoulder bag that can be held securely.
- Take extra care when in crowded areas.
- A discreet money belt inside your clothing is worthwhile.
- Keep to populated areas. Avoid deserted streets at night.

Telephone

To dial an international number use *00* prefix plus country code. Ireland's international country code is *353*. Directory enquiries are ☏ *11811* or ☏ *11850*. The emergency number for police, ambulance or fire is ☏ *999* or ☏ *112*.

Tax-Free Shopping

You are eligible to receive a VAT (sales tax) refund on purchased goods if you live outside the European Union. Shops display a sticker. Refunds at the refund desk at Dublin Airport.

Time

Ireland shares the same time-zone as the UK. In winter it is on Greenwich Mean Time (GMT). In the summer it is GMT plus 1hr.

Tipping

Usually no tipping in pubs, unless you are being served at table. 10% is a good guide for services like restaurants and taxis, but only if you get good service.

Toilets

Fir and *Mná*, in Irish, mean 'men' and 'women', respectively.

Tourist Information

Dublin Discover Ireland Centre, Suffolk St, D2. ☏ *01 6057700.*
College Green Tourism Office, 37 College Green, D2. ☏ *01 4100700.*
Dublin's Tourist Office, 33 Bachelor's Walk, D1. ☏ *01 8723333.*
Tourism Office, 69 O'Connell St, D1. ☏ *086 0216063.*

Dublin Timeline

To 1000 AD

Half-way along the east coast of Ireland is a C-shaped bay, which offers shelter. Mesolithic shore-dwellers settled around 5000 BC and in succeeding millennia Neolithic and Bronze Age settlements grew up.

c. 350 BC Celts arrive. Celtic place-names like Rathfarnham (*Ráth Fearnáin*) and Rathmines (*Ráth Maonais*) are from this era.

c. AD 140 The geographer Ptolemy refers to a settlement called Eblana, possibly around Dublin Bay.

c. AD 450 St Patrick visits and carries out baptisms in St Patrick's Well (near the present St Patrick's Cathedral).

AD 770 Reference is made to a ford across the river Liffey – Dublin's name in Irish, *Baile Átha Cliath*, originates from *Áth Cliath* (the ford of hurdles).

AD 837 Vikings (of Norwegian origin) sail into Dublin Bay. They set up a trading fort near where the River Poddle flows into the Liffey, called *Dubh Linn* (black pool) – hence the name Dublin in English.

AD 902 The King of Leinster attacks and expels the Vikings from Dublin.

AD 917 Vikings (now from Denmark) return. They decisively defeat the Irish High King. Now an important trading town is established, located around the present site of Dublin Castle.

AD 997 Coins are minted in Norse Dublin, the first in Ireland.

1000-1200

1014 The Irish High King Brian Ború defeats the Vikings and Leinstermen in the bloody Battle of Clontarf. After the battle, Brian is slain by a Viking chief.

1169 A small expeditionary Norman force lands in Co Wexford. In summer 1170, a stronger force, led by Richard FitzGilbert de Clare (Strongbow) takes Dublin.

1172 Henry II visits Ireland, spending three months in Dublin. He confirms Strongbow as Lord of Leinster.

1185 Prince John, Lord of Ireland, spends nine months in Dublin.

1191 Construction of St Patrick's Cathedral starts.

1200-1400

1204 King John orders the construction of a castle in Dublin.
1209 The need for fortifications is proven when 500 settlers, at leisure outside the city walls, are massacred by men from Wicklow in Cullen's Wood (present-day Ranelagh).
1348 Dublin is ravaged by the Black Death.
1394 King Richard II visits Dublin.

1400-1600

1487 Anglo-Irish lords support the crowning of the 10-year old pretender Lambert Simnel as King of England in Christ Church Cathedral. Simnel and his army are later routed in England.
1537 King Henry VIII orders the dissolution of the monasteries in Ireland – 10 are seized in Dublin.
1548 Protestantism is pronounced as the official religion in Ireland.
1591 Red Hugh O'Donnell (son of the lord of Donegal) escapes from prison in Dublin Castle.
1592 Establishment of Trinity College (on the site of a former monastery) by Queen Elizabeth I, intended to educate the sons of the Irish elite in accordance with the tenets of Protestantism.

1600-1700

1601 The Elizabethan conquest is completed with the defeat of the Irish lords at the Battle of Kinsale.
1647 Dublin is embroiled in the English Civil War and a Parliamentary force takes the city.
1649 Royalist forces attack Dublin but are routed at the Battle of Rathmines. Cromwell arrives in Dublin with a large force. Not a man of great subtlety, he proceeds to stable his horses in St Patrick's Cathedral. He eliminates all opposition across Ireland and follows this by vigorous ethnic cleansing. His soldiers are granted confiscated land.
1660 The Restoration: Charles II is crowned King.
1662 The Duke of Ormonde is appointed Lord Lieutenant. He begins an energetic development of Dublin. The quays are expanded and the Phoenix Park is laid out.

Dublin Timeline

1680 The Royal Hospital in Kilmainham is begun on the site of an old monastery.
1685 The Catholic James II becomes king, to be overthrown by the Protestant William of Orange in 1688. In 1689, James arrives in Ireland to rally his supporters.
1690 William's forces enter Ireland from the north and at a battle on the river Boyne on 11 July 1690, the Jacobite forces are defeated. James flees and King William enters Dublin two days later. He attends a thanksgiving service in St Patrick's Cathedral.
1691 The defeat of the Jacobite forces is marked by the Treaty of Limerick. The treaty is soon broken and penal laws, which set severe restrictions on Catholics and Dissenters, are introduced.

1700-1800

Dublin's century of rapid development has begun. Dublin is to end the 18th century as the second city, after London.
1701 The Royal (now Collins) Barracks is begun, with the largest barracks square in Europe.
1701 Marsh's Library is founded by Archbishop Marsh.
1713 Jonathan Swift is appointed Dean of St Patrick's Cathedral
1729 Construction begins of Parliament House in College Green.
1730 Henrietta St, dubbed the grandest street in Dublin, is begun by Luke Gardiner, property developer *par excellence*.
1742 The first performance of Handel's *Messiah* takes place in the Musick Hall in Fishamble St.
1745 Leinster House, the grandest house in Dublin, is built. The centre of gravity of Georgian Dublin shifts south of the Liffey.
1757 The Wide Streets Commission is established, and has a seminal role in the development of the grand streets and vistas of Georgian Dublin.
1758 The Casino in Marino is commenced for the Earl of Charlemont to a design by William Chambers.
1759 Arthur Guinness establishes his brewery at St James's Gate. The Grand Canal reaches Dublin, terminating at a harbour near James's St.
1781 The Custom House is begun, to a design by James Gandon.

1784 Sackville St (later O'Connell St) is laid out by the Wide Streets Commission
1785 James Gandon's Four Courts begins construction.
1789 The Royal Canal is completed, terminating at Broadstone Harbour. A year later the Grand Canal loops around the south of the city to reach the Liffey.
1798 A rebellion flares up around the country, with wholesale slaughter on both sides. In Dublin, the rebel Lord Edward Fitzgerald is arrested. The leader of the United Irishmen, Wolfe Tone is captured and brought to Dublin. Sentenced to death, he commits suicide.

1800-1900

1800 The authorities, frightened of rebellion, induce the Irish Parliament to vote to abolish itself. The Act of Union takes effect in January of the following year, when the parliamentarians move from Dublin to London.
1803 A small rebellion led by Robert Emmet in Dublin is easily suppressed. Emmet is captured and executed. At his trial he makes a stirring speech which ends *When my country takes her place among the nations of the earth, then and not till then, let my epitaph be written.*
1815 Work begins on the Catholic Pro-Cathedral, set in the relative obscurity of Marlborough St.
1821 King George IV visits Dublin. He departs from Dunleary which was renamed 'Kingstown' for the occasion.
1829 Catholic Emancipation ends last formal restrictions on Catholics.
1834 The Dublin & Kingstown Railway is opened, the world's first suburban railway. By 1865 Dublin is connected by rail to most Irish cities and towns.
1835 St Paul's Church in Arran Quay is built. Classical and imposing, it is one of many prominent Catholic churches constructed in the city in these decades.
1845-52 The Great Irish Famine. Dublin is not directly affected but swarms of starving people flock to the poorhouses of the city. Soup

kitchens are set up.
1849 Queen Victoria visits Dublin. She visits again in 1853 and 1861. It will be 39 years before she returns again.
1854 Oscar Wilde is born at Westland Row. Two years later, George Bernard Shaw is born in Synge St.
1864 The National Gallery of Ireland is opened. Other great Dublin institutions open during the 19th century: The Natural History Museum (1857), the National Museum and the National Library (1890).
1867 The Fenians (who believed in gaining Irish independence by force) rebel. There are ineffectual skirmishes in Tallaght near Dublin and the rebellion fizzles out.
1882 James Joyce is born in Rathgar, D6.
1886 Guinness Brewery is the largest brewery in the world.

1900-2000

1900 Queen Victoria visits Dublin, her last visit. She stays for three weeks.
1905 Founding of Sinn Féin
1913 The Irish Volunteers are set up by nationalist leaders including Patrick Pearse.
1916 Central Dublin is seized by insurgents. The proclamation of the Irish Republic is read out outside the GPO. The British military, with troops and artillery, supress the rebellion within a week. Hundreds are killed and O'Connell St is devastated. Soon afterwards, the rebel leaders are executed in Kilmainham Gaol.
1918 Sinn Féin gains majority of parliamentary seats in Ireland in the General Election.
1919 The first Dáil Éireann (Irish Parliament) meets in the Mansion House. A guerrilla war by the IRA against British rule ensues and lasts for two years.
1921 The Anglo-Irish Treaty is signed.
1922 Irish nationalists split over whether to accept the Treaty. Anti-Treaty forces occupy the Four Courts. The new Free State Government shells the Four Courts and the Civil War begins. After the capture of the Four Courts, fighting spreads to O'Connell Street

which is devastated once again. Anti-Treaty forces disperse from Dublin and the war continues across the country.
1923 The bitter Civil War is concluded in May, with the Free State Government victorious.
1923 W. B. Yeats is awarded the Nobel Prize for literature. George Bernard Shaw is awarded the prize two years later.
1932 Fianna Fáil win general election. Eamon de Valera (former Anti-Treaty leader) becomes leader of the country.
1939 Ireland remains neutral during the Second World War (which was called the 'Emergency').
1941 German bombs are dropped on Dublin, resulting in 37 people being killed.
1949 The Republic of Ireland is established
1959 Seán Lemass becomes *Taoiseach* (Prime Minister). In due course the economy begins to grow.
1963 President John F. Kennedy visits Dublin.
1966 The Nelson Pillar is blown up by an IRA faction in March.
1966 Celebrations of the 50th anniversary of the Easter Rising.
1974 Car bombs, planted by northern loyalists, explode in Dublin: 25 killed.
1979 Visit by Pope John Paul II. A million people assemble in Phoenix Park.
1987 Legislation is passed to set up the International Financial Services Centre in Dublin's docklands.

2000 to Present

The Celtic Tiger has begun to roar and Dublin grows. Cranes dot the skyline. Apartments and office blocks are built all over the city, many of dubious quality.
2001 Farmleigh House, purchased by the State from the Guinness family, is opened to the public.
2004 Dublin's light rail system, the *Luas*, opens.
2008 to the present. The Celtic Tiger collapses. In the recession years that follow, the building boom has ended and the economy struggles. Despite this, Dublin is resilient and its unique charm and spirit prevail.

Dublin Sights

There is a Dublin tradition (juvenile, irreverent or scatological, or all three?) of giving statues and monuments alternative names.

Anna Livia
Relocated from O'Connell St to near Wolfe Tone Quay. *'The floozie in the jacuzzi'; 'The hoor in the sewer'*. ('Hoor' is colloquial for 'whore')

James Joyce
North Earl St, D1, just off O'Connell St. *'The prick with the stick'*.

Luas
The Green Line of the light rail system runs through the impeccably-affluent south Dublin suburbs. *'The choo-choo for the too-few'*.

Molly Malone
At College Green, kitsch figure from the song 'Molly Malone'. *'The tart with the cart'; 'The dolly with the trolley'; 'The dish with the fish'*.

Convention Centre Dublin
North Wall Quay. Sparkling new convention centre with tilted and curved glass frontage. *'The drum out of plumb.'*

Oscar Wilde
Fine statue on a rock in Merrion Square. *'The queer with the leer'; 'The fag on the crag'*.

The Spire
Also known as 'Monument to Light' in O'Connell Street. *'The stiletto in the ghetto'; 'The stiffy at the Liffey.'*

Women on a bench
Liffey St, north of the Ha'penny Bridge. *'The hags with the bags.'*

Index

Credits

Thanks are due to Veronica Barry and Patrick Sammon for their help in producing this guidebook.

Feedback

Things change. We welcome feedback (suggestions, corrections) so that we can update and improve the next edition. Please send to *info@andalus.ie*.